# Scream Queen

Also by Yvette Fielding:

*Most Haunted Theatres*

THE GHOST HUNTER CHRONICLES
*The House in the Woods*
*The Ripper of Whitechapel*
*The Witches of Pendle*

# Scream Queen

# YVETTE FIELDING

*A memoir*

EBURY
SPOTLIGHT

Ebury Spotlight, an imprint of Ebury Publishing
20 Vauxhall Bridge Road
London SW1V 2SA

Ebury Spotlight is part of the Penguin Random House group of companies
whose addresses can be found at global.penguinrandomhouse.com

Penguin
Random House
UK

First published by Ebury Spotlight in 2024

www.penguin.co.uk

A CIP catalogue record for this book is available from the British Library

ISBN 9781529929140

Printed and bound in Great Britain by Clays Ltd, Elcograf S.p.A.

The authorised representative in the EEA is Penguin Random House
Ireland, Morrison Chambers, 32 Nassau Street, Dublin D02 YH68.

Penguin Random House is committed to a sustainable future for
our business, our readers and our planet. This book is made
from Forest Stewardship Council® certified paper.

MIX
Paper | Supporting
responsible forestry
FSC® C018179

*For my pops, Eric Torevell. A kind, beautiful soul and a true hero – not just as a soldier, but as a husband, father, grandfather, great-grandfather and friend.*

*Love you Pops.*

# CONTENTS

# FOREWORD

It's 1987 and I'm presenting *Blue Peter* with Caron Keating. One day, we are both asked to sit in and watch the final auditions to find a replacement for Janet Ellis and to give our thoughts.

I honestly can't remember who else was auditioning that day, but I do remember this young, natural, fun girl with red hair and a Manchester accent. When it came to the point in the audition where she had to make something (in true *Blue Peter* style), she totally came alive and lost herself in the process. Her enthusiasm was infectious. Caron and I looked at each other and said, 'She's great.' The girl was Yvette Fielding, and she got the job.

As you will read in this book, Yvette found her first year on the show very difficult. Eighteen-year-old Yvette was away from home for the first time in her life and she found living and working in London very tough. Having never presented live television before, she was suddenly thrust into the pressure of fronting, twice a week, the most popular and famous children's television programme ever. Despite all the many personal and public challenges during this time, Yvette came through and ended up becoming one of the most well-loved *Blue Peter* presenters.

We laughed so much together. Yvette has never taken herself seriously and is able to find the fun in almost any situation. Caron, Yvette and I were three very different people, but we really clicked as a team. Off camera, the three of us would laugh till we cried, usually over something Yvette had said or done. On screen, we complemented each other. Caron was the trendy, cool, gorgeous journalist with the strong Northern Irish accent. I was the experienced live-telly presenter and actor from Yorkshire who loved to perform. Yvette was, well, simply Yvette. Authentic. She never tried to be anything other than herself. Children and adults alike loved her screams of terror on a rollercoaster ride, laughed with her when she made a total inedible mess cooking a pancake, and shared her sorrow when she met the abandoned orphans in Romania while filming one of the *Blue Peter* appeals.

It is this authenticity that has enabled Yvette and her creation, *Most Haunted*, to be the success that they are. In each episode of her show, she will suddenly scream in shock as a door slams or an object falls to the floor, and we react with her. When she becomes genuinely petrified in a scary situation, we truly feel her fear because it's for real.

Over the years, many people have asked me which qualities I think make a good television or radio presenter. I always say the same thing – a genuine ability to be yourself, to be who you really are. Yvette has had this quality since that first *Blue Peter* audition and she's never lost it.

# FOREWORD

Fame and fortune haven't altered who Yvette is in any way. She will tell you what she honestly thinks. She's considerate, modest, slightly shy, daft as a brush (as we say Up North) and the most generous, genuine friend anyone could wish for.

Yvette has come such a long way since we first met in 1987 and she totally deserves every bit of her success.

*Mark Curry, 2024*

# INTRODUCTION

I first met Yvette one sweltering night in early July 2005 when she brought the *Most Haunted* team to investigate the old *Coronation Street* set in the centre of Manchester. I was then just one year into what would turn out to be a 17-year career on the creative team of the soap, culminating in my becoming the senior storyline writer for several years. That old set, which was built on an ancient graveyard, was always eerily atmospheric. Few who worked there doubted it was haunted and many, me included, had experienced odd happenings over the years ranging from taps and footsteps to the occasional full apparition.

When I heard that Yvette was bringing her team to investigate the site I was keen to join other *Corrie* cast and crew members on the investigation because I'd been a fan of *Most Haunted* right from the start. As with other *Most Haunted* investigations, this went through the night, right until 5 the next morning, so the teams from both shows had plenty of time to get to know each other. Yvette and I clicked the moment we met. Maybe it's because we have a lot in common. We're both northerners and share the same sense of humour. We've also both worked on national tele-vision institutions and met some wonderful people there. As well as some who were rather less so. We even both share a love of Morecambe and Wise. I also met Karl Beattie that night in 2005 and you cannot talk about Yvette for long without mentioning Karl. Theirs is a marriage rooted in deep love and mutual respect; one that allowed them to create a show that has been sold to over 100 countries and was built on the solid foundations of their good humour, decency and humanity.

When I finally stepped off the soap treadmill a couple of years ago, Yvette asked if I'd be interested in working with her on this memoir. I jumped at the chance because our friendship has grown stronger over two decades. I'm so glad she asked me because although I obviously knew about her journey from being the youngest ever *Blue Peter* presenter to arguably the most famous paranormal investigator in the world, it's been a privilege to learn so much more about her life and those people who've been such an influence on her, not least her remarkable grand-parents. Every industry has its share of bullies and backstabbers, and Yvette and I have both learned over the years that television, perhaps, has more than most. Even so, I've been shocked by Yvette's recollections of the awful behaviour she's faced in her career, and can only admire the way she's risen above it all with grace and a remarkable capacity for forgiveness.

That old *Coronation Street* site where we first met was abandoned to its ghosts in 2013 when the production moved to a shiny but soulless new set in MediaCity, and it was finally demol-ished a few years later. But *Most Haunted* in all its various forms

INTRODUCTION

marches on, undeniably stronger than ever. There's much more to Yvette than *Most Haunted*, of course, and here she tells the story of her unique life and career with wit and candour. A story that has at its heart an enduring and inspiring love story.

*Martin Sterling, 2024*

# Chapter 1

# THE HORROR OF PENDLE HELL

*D*O YOU BELIEVE IN GHOSTS? When people ask me that question, I always tell them honestly that, yes, I do. There's a very simple reason for this: seeing is believing, and for the past 25 years I have encountered hundreds of them with my wonderful husband, Karl Beattie, through our show, *Most Haunted*. I can't think there are many people who would choose 'ghost hunting' as their preferred career option when leaving school. I know I certainly didn't, but I have loved every second of it. I've been exposed to every gamut of human emotion in the places I've investigated and through the spirits I've met. I've experienced moments of terror and intense sadness. Of joy and playfulness. Not to mention flashes of unintentional hilarity.

My story is also the story of *Most Haunted*. Not only did the show become a global phenomenon, but it's been part of my life for almost the whole length of my marriage and has shaped the core beliefs I hold today. In this memoir, I want to reveal to you how the journey of my life led me to create the show with Karl, as well as everything that my search for the truth about the paranormal has taught me about myself.

I begin with the investigation that fans ask me about more than any other, even though it was broadcast two decades ago, on

# Chapter 1

the last weekend of October 2004. The first location we'd investigated that really left me feeling totally and utterly bewildered by what I'd witnessed and the one that disturbs me to this day.

That place is the dark, ominous and very foreboding Pendle Hill.

*   *   *

The towering Pendle Hill rises like a gravestone from the peaceful valleys of Lancashire, dominating the landscape and casting a looming shadow of dread across everyone who sees it. The area has been the epicentre of paranormal activity in the area for more than a thousand years. Ghosts, monsters, unexplained lights and sounds, and horrific creatures dominate the local histories and mythology of the nearby villages.

But the 'Pendle Witches' story is the most notorious of the legends in this location. It was here that a group of 12 local people, mostly but not exclusively female, were ruthlessly and savagely tried and executed for witchcraft in Jacobean times. Most of the so-called Pendle Witches weren't witches at all. They were instead innocent and misunderstood 'cunning women' – the wise women of the villages who merely practised folk medicine and were caught up in the general moral panic in the wake of the Gunpowder Plot of 1605. In fact, one of those hanged as a witch, a wealthy and educated woman named Alice Nutter, was found guilty and sentenced to death only by association even though her connection with the other accused was tenuous. The only one of those tried who admitted to being a true witch was Elizabeth Demdike, who was put in a cell in horrible conditions in Lancaster prison. She died there, unlike the others who were all found guilty of witchcraft (although they denied it) and were hanged. Even now, more than 400 years later, many local people will only talk about this dark part of their history in hushed tones. Yet it's this history that generates much of its tourism.

Pendle Hill still gives off a sense of bleak sadness and dark fear even to this day. It is, without doubt, one of the most haunted places in Britain. And it was here that I took the *Most Haunted Live* team to investigate for our tenth live show.

We've always looked forward to our lives. What we see is truly what you see – as it happens. Sometimes nothing does happen and those are the times when I'm reminded that fronting three hours or more of live television is a very big void to fill! But that wouldn't be the case this time.

By this stage, the *Most Haunted* team was quite a large and well-oiled machine. We'd been working together for some time and shared some incredible experiences, although it must be said some of the team were still sceptical that ghosts existed. Our sound recordist, Jon Gilbert, was especially unconvinced. He's a big, tough guy who's been to war zones, been shot at and seen people killed; in other words, he's been to lots of frightening places that have nothing to do with the paranormal. He'd done five regular *Most Haunted* shows with us, but this was his first live one. It was an assignment he, and we, would never forget.

We were due to investigate Pendle Hill across three nights. On the first, we investigated Clitheroe Castle, which was built on a limestone outcrop in 1186. It's been the scene of much bloodshed over the centuries and has its fair share of reported ghosts.

## Chapter 1

There's a spectral monk, who drifts along a pathway, his head bowed and his hands clasped, as he softly chants; there's the ghost of a handsome man who was hanged for murdering his mistress and his wife, and who reportedly wakes local people regularly by shouting and singing; and there are alleged to be three Royalist officers, who were executed in 1647, wandering around seeking redemption.

That first night was lively enough and we picked up quite a bit of activity and evidence. But that was just a prelude, a softening up even, for everything that was about to be hurled at us on night two. A night that, at times, I wasn't even sure I'd come through unscathed.

We kicked off the night at Lower Wellhead Farm with plans to travel to Bull Hole Valley and Tynedale Farm later in the evening. We'd picked these locations because it was allegedly where the Pendle Witches had lived. The whole team was cautious about the night ahead as this was the first time we'd investigated witchcraft. So there was something dark and malevolent about the whole night even before we'd begun. It wasn't helped by one medium warning that 'they' would be waiting for me there. And by 'they', I was assuming he meant the Pendle Witches.

Lower Wellhead Farm gave us an inauspicious welcome when we heard some local dogs howling nearby. My husband Karl thought he'd seen someone in one of the upstairs windows while I was filming my first piece to camera but, when he checked, all the crew were accounted for and downstairs.

The moment we stepped inside that house a horrible, negative feeling, almost of revulsion, washed over me and I felt incredibly cold. Catherine Howe, who was our make-up artist at the time and the one who stayed with us the longest, was having a look round with Karl when a door was pushed out of her hand, which made her scream. I really didn't like that place at all; it felt like someone was watching me the whole time. It was a relief, albeit temporarily, to move on to the next location: Tynedale Farm. Had we known what was about to happen to us, we'd have stayed where we were.

Tynedale Farm was a bleak, tiny little farmhouse down a dirt track in the middle of nowhere. No one quite knows the precise history of it. Alice Nutter, one of the alleged witches, is thought to have lived there and some of the others who were condemned might have visited. It was owned by a local family, who swore that it was full of spirits and presences. They'd experienced lights, bangs and screams throughout the house. They hated that place and hadn't lived in it for 20 years. Nor would any local venture anywhere near it after dark. When we visited, the house was practically derelict and the front door barely attached. Andy Lynch, who was our head of security and safety on some of our live shows, wouldn't even let the investigation team into certain parts because of missing floorboards and decaying walls, which were liable to collapse. But I believe you can Airbnb it now if you really fancy scaring yourself to death.

\* \* \*

I was already in a heightened state of anticipation when my van pulled up outside, with other members of the team in a van behind. Was this just because I'd been ramping myself up mentally about this place all day, as the parapsychologist who was our resident sceptic might say, or was it something more sinister? I remember getting out, standing in about four inches of mud, and looking at this cheerless and wretched little house in the dark. My stomach suddenly turned over. I felt sick and I started to physically shake. I knew that this side of the valley had a chequered paranormal history, with frequent reported sightings of monks and a woman in grey, but it was this small house that was notorious as being where most activity took place.

By the time we were ready to go on air, we had the main night-vision camera set up, plus other little cameras around. The team numbered around ten people; with just one bedroom and a bathroom upstairs, and a front room, corridor and kitchen on the ground floor, there would be quite a lot of us fitting into this small house.

As soon as we opened the door to start the live broadcast I admit I was absolutely petrified. My mouth was dry and I was physically shaking. The atmosphere was electric. It just didn't feel like a good place. In fact, it was horrible and nasty. I felt I had to have someone in front of me, behind me and at either side. I just didn't want to have any empty space around me.

Almost immediately, strange activity kicked off. The electricity meter, which was in the hallway on the left-hand side as you opened the door, was whizzing round despite not being connected to the mains. I was amazed when I saw it, but it wasn't the first time I'd seen ghosts and paranormal activity interfering with electricity. I thought to myself, *Okay, so we've walked into a haunted location and now something's messing with the electrics.* I knew we weren't alone, which added to my stress levels. As we were trying to get our heads round the electricity meter, we suddenly heard a woman's laughter. It sounded harsh. Threatening. I was already concerned about how much trouble we'd be in.

Karl and Stuart Torevell, who was our rigger, ventured down into the cellar. Right from the start of *Most Haunted*, the team has separated on investigations to cover all bases. Also, if we're all in the same room and I call out, 'Do something to Karl or Stuart,' nothing happens. If they're in another room, however, it often does. Karl and Stuart thought they saw a strange shape in the cellar, and Stuart admitted he felt very uncomfortable down there.

Some of us heard shuffling noises and whispering in our ears, which we couldn't explain. Then our cameraman Jon Dibley started to feel unwell. 'Are you okay, Jon?' I asked.

'I feel so sick,' he said. 'My head is banging.'

This didn't surprise me. People often feel sick during paranormal investigations. It's all to do with energy. Negative energy can make you feel nauseous and dizzy; sometimes you can even faint and collapse. I felt certain that whoever, or whatever, was in that house wanted us to get out.

'How's everyone else feeling?' I asked.

'Do you want the truth?' Stuart said. 'I'm fucking petrified. What I saw down in the cellar wasn't nice at all.'

I then saw that Jon really wasn't looking good. 'Are you sure you're all right?' I checked.

'Not really,' he replied. 'I've suddenly got a really sore throat.'

I told him he could go outside if he'd prefer, but Jon is a true professional and insisted on carrying on.

I suggested we do a Ouija board session to try to find out what was going on. As we sat down, I had no idea the next hour would be one that none of us would ever forget.

Although the audience watching at home could see us with the night-vision cameras, we were sitting in the pitch black. We couldn't see our hands in front of our faces. The only tiny source of illumination came from the lights on top of the cameras.

With our fingers on top of the glass, I called out to ask who was there.

'Please come forward. Please try.'

The temperature suddenly dropped around my legs, something that showed up clearly on the thermal imaging camera. The table trembled slightly and then Karl complained of feeling odd.

'It's hard to explain,' he said. 'I feel drained. It's like one minute I'm here and the next your voice is just like a distant echo.'

I asked if he wanted to carry on, but he insisted that he wanted to see where this took us.

I called out again: 'Let us know you're here. Can you move the table for us in any way? Move this glass. Touch one of us if you can.'

Another cold breeze crossed my hand and Karl complained of feeling frozen.

The table started to move more, lifting off the floor slightly, almost as though it were floating.

'Please make the table move more violently if you can,' I asked, 'so that we know you're here.'

I could see my breath in front of my face in the tiny light coming from the top of the night-vision camera as the table moved more definitely.

'Make the glass move. Bang one of the doors in the house. Whisper in our ears. Show us some lights.'

We all heard creaking. The table moved some more. Then I sensed Karl really wasn't well. When I asked if he was okay, his answer was feeble and almost inaudible. I asked him if he wanted to step outside but, like Jon Dibley, he insisted on staying. A couple more of the team were now reporting feeling lightheaded.

The glass now started to become active and was moving more violently than I've ever known. I tried to use this activity to ascertain who was communicating with us. There were, according to the Ouija board, nine spirits in that room with us. But there was one dominant presence coming through.

Was it a male?

No.

I tried some of the names of the alleged Pendle Witches.

'Is your name Alice?'

Another no.

Eventually I tried the name Elizabeth.

This time I got confirmation.

'Were you considered a witch, Elizabeth?'

Yes, again.

So this was Elizabeth Demdike. The only one who had admitted to being a witch.

'Can you see us, Elizabeth?' I asked.

There was sharp knocking underneath the table in response. Knocking and tapping are very prevalent in hauntings. They are one of the many ways spirits communicate. They can knock two for yes and one for no if you ask a direct question or, if you're using a Ouija board, the spirit might knock when it wants you to stop at a certain letter of the alphabet to spell out messages. It's all to do with energy and is an excellent way of communicating.

'We need more from you, Elizabeth,' I insisted. 'We're not leaving unless you tell us to leave. Use all our energies to let us know you want us to go.'

There was instant banging all around us. This is something else we experience regularly. Often I feel it under my feet or hear it in the walls, and sometimes it sounds as though someone is running above me on the ceiling. For me, the worst is when I can actually feel the vibration through my feet. And the louder it is, the more scared I get. The louder the spirit, the more energy it has. It leaves me wondering what else the spirit will be capable of.

This banging was very loud indeed.

The table started shaking and lifting. Cath reported that she, too, now felt sick. Then Andy, who is as matter-of-fact as they come, said he felt a deep breath on his neck.

I could hear a squeaking noise and couldn't quite discern what it was at first. It was coming from under the table. And then I worked out just what that sound was.

I could hear an unseen hand loosening the screws.

The table wobbled and we all heard a woman's laughter. As we struggled to steady the table and start the Ouija session again, I asked Elizabeth if she hated us and if she enjoyed being nasty. The glass scorched around the Ouija board so fast that some of us had to fight to keep our fingers on top of it.

Then Jon Gilbert, our soundman, started panicking as he panted for air. I could see him grasping at his neck as if something was round it and his mouth was open. His eyes were bulging. He looked like a stranded fish.

'What's the matter, Jon?' I cried out. 'What's up?'

'I can't breathe,' he gasped. 'Something's round my neck.'

It was horrible to see this big man gurgling, struggling to breathe, and on the verge of collapse. He's down-to-earth and very professional. He would never mess about on a live broadcast. Andy wanted to get him out of there as soon as possible, if only to ascertain there wasn't some rational explanation, such as him having accidentally got a cable trapped round his neck.

As Andy led Jon outside, Stuart collapsed, complaining that a rope was strangling him. He was making horrible guttural sounds, as if he was being sick. And, in fact, we later discovered that he had vomited. Stuart is my friend and colleague, but also my cousin. Seeing him on the ground, not being able to breathe, was horrifying. I remember becoming almost hysterical and screaming out for a medic. Having just taken Jon Gilbert outside, Andy rushed back and, being a first aider, he dragged Stuart out.

Now it was Cath's turn. She felt terrible. Her legs buckled and she fainted. She, too, was bundled out, a little unceremoniously, as Andy scooped her up and carried her away.

Three down. It was awful to watch them drop like flies and I went outside to make sure they were okay. Paramedics had been called and I was distraught to see my friends and colleagues lined up on the floor being given emergency treatment. Stuart had clearly been affected the worst. He was unconscious. His lips were blue, his eyes had rolled back and they were struggling to bring him round.

But I knew we were in the middle of a live broadcast, albeit with a depleted team, so I went back inside Tynedale Farm to resume the Ouija board session. I goaded Elizabeth to do more. I knew this was unwise. However, this was incredible activity we were getting and it's what we'd come for. Getting proof like this is the whole reason we make *Most Haunted*. So despite all the fear I was feeling and my concern for my colleagues and friends, I also knew at the back of my mind this was going out live. It was something unique and I had to make the best of the situation.

'You're only taking us one at a time,' I told Elizabeth. 'You need to take all of us to get us out of here. So how are you going to do that? Lift this table off the floor. Scare us all to death and we'll never come back.'

The glass started moving in a frenzy again. I asked it to point out who would be affected next. It pointed at Karl.

An icy breeze swept round us and I noticed Karl was very quiet. He complained of feeling frozen again. I was suddenly very worried about him. I told him to get outside to take a break. He refused. He was stubbornly fighting whatever was doing this to him. He had come to this place to investigate and so investigate he would.

The table was now moving violently and I wondered what the people watching at home and the studio audience were making of all this. I couldn't think where this was going to end. The situation started to get to Sally Matthews, our floor manager, and as I tried to calm her down, it finally became too much for Karl. As Andy guided him out, Jon Dibley put his head back and then collapsed. The camera slipped from his hands and crashed onto the floor.

Karl had known Jon for around 12 years by this stage. They'd worked together on just about every kind of TV show going. Jon is about as sceptical as you can imagine. But here he was in a haunted house, half-conscious and clearly struggling to breathe.

After Andy helped Jon out, that left just three of us standing – me, Sally and our then parapsychologist. I heard screaming in my ear.

'Someone pick up the camera!'

It was the studio hub. The camera was on the floor and the network had lost all pictures.

'There's no one left,' Sally said.

'We need pictures!' they shouted.

Sally, who'd never picked up a TV camera in her life, grabbed hold of it and between us we managed to put back all the leads and cables that had been ripped out when Jon fell. Sally acted as our cameraperson for the remaining minutes of the show.

I was in tears when we came off-air. An absolute wreck. I couldn't make sense of what had happened. All I knew was that I had witnessed my friends and colleagues being assaulted and picked off one by one. And the most frightening thing of all was that they all described it later as feeling as though they were being strangled. And when I looked at their necks, they all had red marks around them.

Marks that looked just like they'd been strangled by a rope.

\* \* \*

Even watching that footage 20 years later sends a shiver down my spine. I know some doubters have claimed that we were acting it all out. But we weren't. It was genuine. For some reason that I don't understand, I wasn't affected. But it was very real and I was terrified.

To this day, I can't explain what happened that night. Our parapsychologist suggested afterwards that it was a form of mass hysteria. That's certainly one possible explanation, and I would be the first to admit we all had a sense of heightened awareness and fear when we arrived at Tynedale Farm.

But since some of those affected were complete sceptics, I would submit that's unlikely. Nor would mass hysteria explain the red marks I saw.

Hundreds of people still trek across that bleak landscape just to take photographs of the place where the *Most Haunted* team fell. It had been just three short years since Karl and I decided to embark on investigating the dead. My first experience of death, though, had happened many years earlier.

## Chapter 2

# FROM SYRIA WITH LOVE

*M*Y FIRST EXPERIENCE OF DEATH came, like most children, with the loss of a beloved pet. For me, it was the demise of Snowy, a beautiful white fluffy rabbit, who was given to me when I was about four or five.

I loved that rabbit so much. But one day, I came home from school and found Mum was waiting for me with a tragic face. 'I'm so sorry, Yvette,' she said, 'but I've something very sad to tell you about Snowy.'

Mum led me to his hutch and when I looked in, Snowy was lying there, not moving. He was quite dead. I cried for a bit, like children do, and that was that. Or so I thought.

Snowy's passing aside, I can only recall my childhood family life as being quite wonderful. It was full of warmth and happiness, marvellous characters and lots of animals. Christmases and birthdays were nothing but joyous family occasions.

I was born at 5.15am on Monday, 23 September 1968, the first child of Angela and Alan Fielding, and I was to remain their only child until the arrival of my brother Rick, 11 years later. Children can often feel resentful when a baby brother or sister comes along. Especially if, like me, they'd had their mum and dad all to themselves for several years. But my reaction was totally different when Rick was born: I was thrilled to have a baby brother and all my mothering instincts kicked in early. I became like this wonderful little nanny to Rick and a great help to Mum. I didn't even mind changing his nappy.

I was close to both my parents and they were terrific. Mum and I had some great times together. She'd teach me how to rock and roll in the front room. And we'd also do acrobatics in there. I was always putting on shows for her. I remember being obsessed with Olga Korbut, the Belarusian Olympic gymnast who represented the Soviet Union, and I thought she was marvellous. I'd put my hair in pigtails, then take two buckets and a plank outside to practise.

Dad liked me being athletic as well. He'd take me to play squash when I got a bit older and I was very good at it. He'd started his own company when I was young and I'm very proud that he was the first person to bring over diamond drilling from the US to the UK. He established a very successful company from nothing. He had a works van, which Mum often used to drive. The problem was that when you went round corners, the doors would fly open. So when Mum put me in the front seat, she'd always tie a piece of rope through the handle of the passenger door, across me, then across the gear stick, and then across her while she was driving. I'll never forget the first time I travelled in that van without the rope with the doors flying open at every turning!

Dad liked to watch *Doctor Who* with me. Or at least he tried to. I was usually hiding behind the sofa, as most kids did in the seventies. People are often surprised when I say I don't like watching horror films these days but I was just the same back then. Even the *Doctor Who* theme music terrified me. I only had to hear it to go scuttling behind the leatherette sofa because I was so frightened. It was really frustrating for him. He'd eventually manage to coax me out to gingerly sit beside him, but I was so unsettled that I kept twitching and, every time I moved, the sofa made a farting sound. No matter how many times he told me to sit still, I couldn't. I was too scared.

I've always been an animal lover so Dad bought me a pony once. I called her Moon. She was like a Thelwell pony and she used to run off with me on her back down the streets of Bramhall, on the edge of Greater Manchester. People became used to this sight and they'd just shrug and say, 'There goes little Yvette again.'

I had no control over Moon at all and it must have been hilarious seeing this little fat thing racing down the street with me on its back trying – and always failing – to rein her in.

I also had a Dobermann Pinscher called Heidi. She was a wonderful dog and went with me everywhere. Even when I was playing out with my mates on the estate where we lived in Bramhall.

Kids always played out on the streets back in the seventies. It's just what we did. We'd play rounders and Kickstone 123. And you stayed out with your mates until the streetlights came on, when you were supposed to go home. If you didn't, you were in big trouble. Dogs used to roam freely round estates, too, so I never had Heidi on a lead. Dad encouraged me to take her wherever I went.

'If you go to that park, you take Heidi,' he'd say. 'Don't go anywhere without her. No one will come near you if she's there.'

## Chapter 2

He was right, too, because Heidi, this great big Dobermann with a studded collar, probably looked quite fierce, even though she was really a big softie. She would often sit outside the school waiting patiently for home time when I would come running out. Heidi wasn't universally popular, though, and the teachers would telephone Mum sometimes:

'Can you come and collect your dog, Mrs Fielding? She's frightening the other children.'

\* \* \*

The other major figures in my childhood were my grandparents, Mary and Eric Torevell. Mary was a remarkable woman. She was Syrian and came from a large well-to-do family in Homs, in the west of the country. They were a Catholic family, and her father was a jeweller and goldsmith. She told me she had a very contented pre-war childhood with her siblings.

When the Second World War broke out, Mary volunteered for the Red Cross and that's how she met Eric, who'd joined the 2nd Battalion of the Cheshire Regiment at just 17 and a half years old in January 1935. Eric stayed in the army for 22 years, rising to the rank of sergeant.

He was posted to Palestine in 1936 after training and I'll never forget the story he told me of what happened to him there in November of that year; a story that would upset him to the day he died.

He was posted to Afula as part of the soldiers guarding the Hijaz railway line from Haifa to the Syrian border, which was being used by Allied Forces. On this particular day, a train was due to pass through carrying Royal Navy personnel, machine guns and cannons known as 'pom-poms' because of the sound they made when they were fired. Eric and his comrades were tasked with patrolling the line. At 6.30 that morning he was standing outside the guard room at the station when an old man with a red flag hurried towards him. Pointing up the track, he shouted 'Bomber!' in Arabic.

Eric alerted his corporal and, together with three other soldiers, they scrambled into a patrol buggy and were guided by the old man to where he'd seen the bomb. Assessing the situation, the corporal ordered the four men to get back in the buggy.

'This is a job for the engineers,' he said.

'I'm an engineer,' Eric said. 'I can do this.'

He about-turned to approach the bomb. This was a lad not yet 20 years old, remember.

Eric gently placed his rifle across the explosive armour-piercing shells, creating a buffer between the pins that were being held back by a wire. He then pulled all the nails out of the bombs and dropped them on the floor. Knowing the bomb was safe, he pulled it off the track. The corporal and the other men joined him, Eric put the bomb in a bag and they all headed back to camp in the car.

It was an act of incredible bravery; my grandad risked his life to save many others. But it was what happened next that upset Eric for the rest of his days.

Arriving back at Afula, the corporal told a senior officer what had happened, and the three other privates told Eric that he should have gone with the corporal to say he was the one who defused the bomb. Later that same day, a Navy train stopped at

Afula on the way back to Haifa. The corporal was in the guard room with the others and picked up the remains of the bomb to hand to the Navy personnel. Eric made to follow but the corporal ordered him to get back.

'I will sort this out,' he said, brusquely.

Eric did as he was told.

A few days later, a Navy train stopped by Afula again. The corporal was presented with an engraved pom-pom shell and given a medal. Eric received nothing. He never went forward and didn't say anything. I'm glad I can finally tell his story now.

I think it's a marvellous thing for a man like Eric to save all those lives and to keep quiet about it, even while he watched another man take all the credit for it. I know it rankled with him, but he wasn't bitter. Still, that's the kind of man Eric was, and I understand fully why my grandmother Mary fell in love with him.

Mary didn't speak a word of English when they met, and Eric was from Macclesfield with the broad accent to match. That was no barrier to their love, though, and she accepted when he suggested she come back to England with him to get married. He was still in the Army, though, so they travelled extensively all over the Middle East until they could settle properly.

Mary and Eric were both such unforgettable characters in my life. Every Saturday, without fail, I would go round to their house and the food Mary had prepared was just amazing; there was always a massive spread of Greek and Syrian cuisine.

She always dressed immaculately and looked like a film star. But if she ever saw you were a little bit sad or down, she'd turn around, look at you and then do something so daft you couldn't help laughing. She had a knack of instantly making anyone feel better. It was because Mary was such a remarkable woman that I named my daughter after her.

She would always cheat at cards when she was playing with her friends. One of my favourite memories was seeing her wink at me, and me looking down to see a winning card hidden between her toes.

Sometimes when I got to my grandparents' house on a weekend, I'd catch Mary singing away in Arabic and I would just think to myself: *My grandma is fantastic.* She did try to teach me to speak and count in Arabic but I can only say 'Shut the door' now. As I get older, I really regret not getting the chance to learn more about her side of the family and Syrian history from her. I would have dearly loved to have visited Homs before it was blown up and obliterated in the civil war that began in 2011.

But when I started working in television Mary strongly advised me not to tell anyone where we came from.

'You must tell everyone we're from Greece,' she insisted.

Although this sounded a bit odd to me, I always trusted her advice, so that's what I did.

It was only many years later that I discovered the real reason why she was so adamant about burying our Syrian past. It turned out that a lot of people weren't terribly welcoming to her when she first arrived in England. Some even called her 'a dirty Arab' to her face. So she was frightened that people would be mean to me once I became a TV face and they discovered I'm a quarter Syrian.

That stayed with me for many years and it's only been in the last ten years or so that I've truly embraced my Syrian heritage.

It's something I'm very proud of.

We all called grandad Eric 'Pops' when we were growing up. He had a large moustache and because he'd been a sergeant in the Army, he had this big booming voice as well.

He used to take me and my cousins out in the back of his bright orange Lada. You could see that car coming from miles away. Regular viewers will know my cousin Stuart Torevell as a key member of the *Most Haunted* family, but he's such a big part of my own family, too. Just like my little brother Rick, I mothered him a bit as a child and was often around playing at his house with his two brothers, Gary and Steven. I always looked out for Stuart and I still do; he remains very dear to me because he's such a sweet man. He's one of the people I can truly rely on.

We'd all arrive at a pub somewhere and as soon as you walked in, there'd be our aunties and uncles gathered. All us kids would be sent outside to sit in the car park with our Salt 'n' Shake crisps and bottles of pop while the adults drank inside.

That's just how life was back in the 1970s in the north. And we really loved it.

Even though my dad's parents played less of a role in my life, I thought his father was marvellous. He was called James but he was Jim to everyone. When I was at stage school I'd go around to see him and he'd say, 'Right, then, what poems have you learned today?'

I'd have to stand up straight and recite a poem. He expected everything to be pronounced properly. Stand up straight; enunciate clearly; be a proper lady. Even though my dad had a bit of a northern twang, he spoke very properly and that was down to Jim.

Jim was a very heavy smoker and eventually died of emphysema but even towards the end he'd sit there with an oxygen mask over his face wanting me to recite poems for him. My dad was very close to him and he was very badly affected by his death.

Jim was lovely but I didn't know his wife, my other grandmother, much at all. She was quite a cold woman, even with my dad when he was growing up, and very distant. I didn't really have anything to do with her.

*　*　*

I was very much a tomboy as a child, always climbing trees and getting into scrapes. My knees were usually covered in scratches and bruises. I was in a gang on our local estate when I was about eight, but I was the only girl in a bunch of boys.

We built a den out of breeze blocks once and I was dead chuffed with it. I stood on top of it proudly when we'd finished and said: 'This is fantastic.'

But then suddenly the boys ganged up on me.

'You're not allowed in our gang any more because you're a girl,' one lad said.

I was affronted. 'No, I'm staying,' I asserted. 'I helped build it.'

The next thing, he scooped up a brick and lobbed it at me. It hit me, landing squarely in my face, and I lost all my front teeth.

I pushed my bike home with its little shopping bag on the front and there was all this blood pouring from my mouth. I dropped my bike outside the house and went in wailing to Mum. She, in turn, had to call Dad and it became quite the drama. In fact, I had to have years of corrective surgery on my mouth and for a while I had gold front teeth put in.

The James Bond film *The Spy Who Loved Me* had just come out and Jaws, the giant villain with steel teeth, was very popular at the time. You can imagine how the other kids made fun of my gold teeth. On the other hand, they allowed me to show off because I was the only kid who could bite into ice cream and not feel the effects.

I also well remember the summer of 1976, which was long and very, very hot. There was a terrible drought and the whole country was like a tinderbox. Around that time there was a series of short, animated public information films for children called *Charley Says* in which a cartoon cat called Charley warned children against various perils, such as falling into water or talking to strangers.

One of the films cautioned against playing with matches.

My friends and I should have listened to Charley. Instead, we started mucking about with matches on the school playing field that summer. I've no idea who brought them but the next thing we knew, the whole pitch was ablaze. As it was the school holidays, there was no one to fetch to help. So we just ran away in panic – and this was a whole gang of us – all scared we were going to be arrested and put in prison.

I could see the playing fields from my bedroom window and I remember racing home and then watching all these fire engines turning up to deal with the big black mass of smoke billowing into the air. I was so ashamed of my part in it and didn't tell anyone I was involved until I was in my late twenties.

A bit like Mum and Snowy the rabbit, in fact.

\* \* \*

Four decades after my beloved first pet passed away, Mum had a guilty confession to make.

I was having a gin and tonic or three with Mum when she felt she finally had to get something off her chest: 'Yvette,' she said, 'I'm sorry, but I killed Snowy. And I feel so bad about it. I've held on to this guilt for all this time.'

She went on to explain how she'd come to accidentally kill my first pet that morning all those years ago. She had decided that Snowy might like being let out of his hutch to enjoy the sunshine as it was such a beautiful day. We had a washing line that ran the length of the garden, with a metal post at either end. In her wisdom, Mum decided to put some thin rope around Snowy's neck and then attach it with a hoop at the top of the washing line. The theory was that Snowy could munch on the grass while moving freely up and down.

What she hadn't counted on, and only realised to her horror three or four hours later when she checked on him, was that poor Snowy had gone round and round at one end of the washing line and garrotted himself.

Mortified, Mum laid Snowy to rest in the hutch and waited, dreading me coming home from school when she'd have to tell me he'd died. But not *how* he'd died, obviously.

It was only when I was in my late forties that she finally felt able to divulge the truth to me of just how she'd killed my beautiful bunny.

Poor Snowy.

With Mum being responsible for my first encounter with death, it seems only fitting that she was also there when I had my first ghost sighting.

*Chapter 3*

# WAKING
# THE DEAD

*I* WAS ABOUT 26 WHEN I SAW MY FIRST GHOST.

It was while I was staying at my mum's house, in a small cul-de-sac in Cheshire. There were only five houses and the main Manchester to London railway line ran behind the gardens. Mum owned a small elderly Jack Russell called Tilly at that time who would often stand at the bottom of the stairs barking at something none of us could see. I was aware this worried Mum but as I wasn't living there at the time I just thought it was unusual.

I was asleep in bed when – and I don't know why – I was suddenly awake and alert. There, standing at the bottom of my bed, was the incredibly detailed image of a soldier. Or I should say *half* a soldier, because he had no legs.

The soldier was young, no more than late teens or early twenties, of normal height and not skinny. He was wearing a brown-green uniform with buttons down the front, and had a Brylcreemed side parting. He had large eyes, which were just staring at me.

The encounter was over quite quickly – a kind of one-Mississippi-two-Mississippi-three-and-gone length of time – and then he just wasn't there.

As you can imagine, I screamed the house down, ran out of the bedroom and jumped into bed with my mum because I was so scared of being alone in that room. Mum was worried and upset for me as she could see how terrified I was.

'You do believe me, don't you?' I kept saying.

'Of course, I do,' she reassured as she hugged me. And she did because she'd had all kinds of problems with that house since she moved in.

She would hear footsteps running up and down the stairs, which was awful for her as she was on her own most of the time. I remember her once calling me at work, terrified about what she'd experienced the previous evening and me having to calm her down. She'd often been woken up by an icy blast passing across her face while she was in bed and sometimes she'd also feel the bedclothes being pulled. Occasionally, she even had the impression of being pulled out of bed herself.

It reached the point where she was turning up at work feeling very upset and distressed. One of her colleagues eventually convinced her to go to the church to tell them what was happening.

The local vicar came round and did a blessing of the house. Sadly, that didn't seem to work as the activity continued much as before.

'I'm still getting these icy blasts,' she told me. 'I think there's something still here.'

The incident with the soldier convinced me that something was really happening in the house. Oddly enough, I hadn't really registered that it was a ghost at the time because I didn't really know what a ghost was. And because he had seemed so lifelike, I started to question myself after the fear had abated and the logical side of my brain kicked in.

Had I imagined it? No. And I knew it wasn't a dream. So, after I'd calmed down from the shock, I started to look for a reason behind the activity in the house.

The house itself wasn't terribly old but it hadn't been lived in properly since the 1970s, and it was now the mid-1990s. There had been many owners across that time, but a strange pattern had developed with its ownership. Many people seemed to have bought it and tried to do it up, but then would suddenly up sticks and leave for no apparent reason. So it was all still very seventies inside as Mum started improving it. This involved a great deal of work going on while pipes were being replaced and installed, and maybe all the bulldozers digging up the ground had stirred something up.

However, I doubted that alone could explain the soldier's presence. I asked around Mum's neighbours if they'd witnessed anything odd. And amazingly enough, they had. Some had been woken up in their own homes with their beds vibrating or being shaken. Others had even seen the same soldier that I had, again just from the waist up. I couldn't believe it.

I asked a local historian about the cul-de-sac and she told me that during the Second World War there had been a tragic accident exactly where our gardens met the rail track. All the trains taking young soldiers from Manchester to London and then on to fight would pass by there. But one young lad did not want to fight and, in desperation, he'd jumped from the train and was killed. The train had cut him in half.

Was that the same soldier I had seen at the foot of my bed? It would seem an odd coincidence if it wasn't.

Seeing the image of that young man really ignited my interest in the paranormal. Other neighbours had seen the same figure, which was the key. I knew something unexplainable had happened, and that scared and intrigued me.

\*   \*   \*

I had been casually interested in the paranormal as a child. I remember Mum and I being really into *Arthur C. Clarke's Mysterious World* on TV, which was a prime-time show first broadcast in 1980. Mum used to buy the magazine that accompanied the series and one month they gave away one of those floppy discs that looked like vinyl records that you'd sometimes get on the front of magazines. This one was called *Voices from the Dead* and it was allegedly the voices of dead people recorded by paranormal researchers. Mum put it on the record player and the house suddenly echoed with these mostly unintelligible and scary noises that terrified both of us.

Mum approached the record player like it was the Devil himself, ripped off the floppy disc and threw it in the bin.

'We're never playing *that* again!' she stated.

Even so, it didn't put Mum off us going to visit mediums or having our tarot cards read, although back then it was only ever for fun. I remember her booking us to see a medium in a pub once when I was in my early twenties, but I wasn't terribly impressed by her.

She wouldn't be the last medium to disappoint me.

I had my own pack of tarot cards from about the age of 16 because my college friend Caz's mother used to read cards. She didn't use tarot cards because she could give you a reading from just an ordinary pack of playing cards. I was so impressed and thought I had to learn how to do that. After I got the hang of it, my mother was always asking me to do readings for her and her friends. This went on until I was well into my twenties.

'Bring your cards, Yvette,' she'd say. 'And can Margaret and Jennifer come, too?'

Margaret and Jennifer were Mum's best friends; they'd come around and we'd all sit with gin and tonics in the garden round this 1970s plastic table and parasol that Mum still had. It was such fun. In between sips of G&T, out would come my cards for an impromptu reading. It would be all 'Oh, that bit's true, isn't it, Margaret?' and 'Yes, she's got that right, Jen.'

Mum and I couldn't resist going to see the fortune tellers whenever we went on holiday, despite having to pay about 25 quid for five minutes even back then.

I recall us going to one who operated out of a caravan, and she told me: 'You're in television.' Well, that bit was accurate, but I'd been on TV since I was 13 and she could have recognised me from there.

But then she added: 'You're going to be in television for a very long time. And it's going to be something to do with this. Something to do with the spirit world.'

I wouldn't set up *Most Haunted* for many years yet, though. That story begins in Cheadle Hulme in Cheshire, just southeast of Manchester, in an old farmhouse – the first house I shared with Karl.

\* \* \*

Karl and I first moved in together in 1999. I hadn't encountered paranormal activity since the incident with the soldier at Mum's house, but that was all to change. Within days of us moving in, our neighbour had come around to ask whether anything strange had been going on in our house as she'd seen a woman on her stairs. I'd experienced very strange happenings at the house myself ever since we moved in. And what she said made perfect sense to me given that some of the events I'd heard and witnessed had been around our stairs, which were parallel to those next door; our two houses had formed one bigger house many years previously, before they'd been split.

One of the most frightening things that happened to me at that house occurred about a year after we moved, on a night while Karl was working away. Our two children, William and Mary, were in bed upstairs and I was watching an episode of *Sex and the City*.

There was an archway through to the kitchen from the living room, but no door. As I watched TV, there was a sudden banging. It sounded as though it was from the cupboard doors, but when I went to investigate I could find no cause of what I'd just heard.

Feeling unsettled and a little scared, I turned off the TV and all the lights, and went upstairs. But as soon as I got into bed, I heard the TV turn itself back on downstairs, with the volume turned up high. I was convinced that someone must have got into the house and I was petrified when I ventured downstairs. But there was no one there. I unplugged the TV and went back to bed, although I didn't sleep much.

For a few weeks, nothing further happened. Until I got into bed one night – as before, the children were asleep – and turned off the light. Immediately I heard footsteps coming up the stairs.

They were heavy steps and I believed they belonged to a man.

I thought Karl might have come home from work earlier than expected and called out to him, but there was no reply.

There was a child's safety gate at the top of the stairs because William and Mary were so young; you had to push a button to release and lift the handle. It always creaked when you did this.

I heard the footsteps reach the top of the stairs before they stopped. Then I heard the unmistakable creak of the handle on the safety gate being lifted.

I had absolutely no thoughts of ghosts or hauntings in my head at all in this moment, just the terrible fear that a burglar had got in and that I had to protect my children at all costs.

In a panic, I reached under the bed where I knew Karl kept an antique samurai sword. (That isn't as odd as it might sound because he trained in martial arts from the age of seven.) I grabbed the sword and, shaking with terror, ventured out of the bedroom fully expecting to confront an intruder in the gloom.

But there was no one there. And the most petrifying thing of all to me was that the safety gate was closed, even though I'd distinctly heard it being opened.

Another odd thing about that house involved our daughter Mary.

She was only tiny when we lived there and we would often hear her late at night or early in the morning chattering away in her room as though she was speaking to someone. Karl or I would go in to see what she was up to and she'd point at something we couldn't see and say a word like 'grandma' or 'Mary'.

There was a fabulous photograph of my late grandmother Mary on the landing. Once, when I was carrying her upstairs, my daughter Mary pointed at the photograph and said the word 'Grandma' again. While this was perplexing, I was also strangely comforted by it because I liked to think that my beloved grandmother was coming to visit her little namesake.

Although everything that was happening to us in that house was scaring me, it had also intrigued me and I started reading books about life after death and near-death experiences. If I closed my eyes in the afternoon for a nap, I'd almost go into a state of meditation.

When I told my neighbour about all this, she told me she was interested in the paranormal as well and regularly meditated at the local Buddhist centre. She invited me along to the next meeting and I met a Buddhist there who was interested to hear about everything I'd experienced at the house.

'It's because you've been reading all these books,' he told me. 'You've been doing all this meditation unguided and you don't know what you're doing. You've opened yourself up to the spirits.'

He offered to come to the house the next day to shut everything down and to cleanse me, after which we should have no further problems.

As he walked round the property, he picked up that there'd been a tragic incident there many years ago. A man, who'd been a drunkard, accidentally started a fire which killed his wife and daughter.

Karl and I didn't think much about this story until a year or so later when my son William was really getting into football and we decided to put some turf in the back garden for him. When we hauled up the York paving slabs, we discovered they'd been covering a hole. And in that hole were loads of old gin bottles. I suddenly recalled what the Buddhist had said.

'I reckon this is where he hid all his empty gin bottles,' I said to Karl. I was really fascinated by this because it was the perfect example of very real history converging with the paranormal. I've loved this whenever it's happened in any of the investigations we've done.

That Buddhist was right: we didn't experience any further strange incidents after his visit. However, we sold the house to a soundman who worked for Granada Television, as I sometimes did. After a few weeks of living there, he got a message to us through a mutual friend.

'You could have told me it was haunted,' he said. 'The cupboard doors keep opening and closing all by themselves ...'

\* \* \*

Our experiences in that house were the beginning of our *Most Haunted* story, but not the inspiration for its creation.

That happened when another friend of ours, a cameraman who also worked for Granada TV, popped round one Sunday evening to drop off some equipment he'd borrowed from us. It was pouring down outside, so I ushered him in for a drink. As we chatted, I casually asked him what he'd been up to and where he'd been filming.

## Chapter 3

'I've just come back from this amazing place in East Sussex called Michelham Priory,' he told us. 'It's fabulous and the property manager, Chris Tuckett, is a lovely guy who's so accommodating. If you know anyone who wants to film anything that requires an old priory or house, tell them to get in touch with Chris because he says they can film there for free.' He then added: 'But be warned. It's also badly haunted. Chris reckons there's at least thirteen ghosts there.'

When he'd gone, I noticed that Karl had gone a bit quiet and I could see from his expression he was thinking about something. When I asked him what was on his mind, he turned to me and asked outright: 'How would you feel about spending a night alone in a haunted house?'

I knew that Karl already believed in ghosts because he'd experienced the spirit of the former owner of a previous house he'd owned moving the furniture around.

'No way!' I asserted.

'Okay, then,' he said. 'What if we did it together and with a camera crew?'

Although the prospect terrified me, it also intrigued me and I thought that if Karl and a camera crew were there I'd be more interested in doing it. 'Yeah, I'd be up for that,' I said.

We'd both seen *The Blair Witch Project* a few days earlier and we'd enjoyed its found-footage style, which created a sense of realism and tension by using handheld cameras, natural lighting and very little staging to create mood and suspense. That prompted another idea.

'What if we filmed it the way they did in *Blair Witch*?' I suggested.

That was it. We were suddenly consumed by this idea and we sat up all night, bouncing ideas off each other for this show. We had sheets of paper all over our bed, coming up with concepts of how it might work. It was almost as though we were possessed to make *Most Haunted* happen.

The initial title we came up with was 'Yvette's Haunting Truths', which, let's be honest, is crappy, although Karl – who's always been so protective of my career – insisted it was good because it had my name in the title.

I had to tell him it wasn't fabulous at all.

The first thing we did was get hold of Chris Tuckett at Michelham Priory to ask whether we could stay the night and film a pilot.

'Absolutely,' he said. 'Come down and spend the night. I'll shut the place down for you to do what you must. Whatever you want or need, just ask.' It was fantastically generous of him.

Next, we had to find a crew from the people we knew in the industry, although we had no money to pay them. So what we did was promise them a crate of beer, free food and a night in a haunted location. The soundman had his own sound equipment and the camera guy had his own camera, so we didn't have to pay for those. The one thing we didn't have was a night-vision camera, but the parapsychologist we'd recruited had one. That was how we were able to make it look so spooky with so little money.

Karl and I had decided early on that we should feature a parapsychologist or sceptic on *Most Haunted* to balance the investigation as we also wanted to use a psychic medium on the show. For the medium, I immediately thought of Derek Acorah, who I'd worked with at Granada Breeze. Breeze was a lifestyle channel launched in 1996 (as Granada Good Life), which had some paranormal programming in among the cookery and health programmes. A show on the channel called *Psychic Livetime* had given Derek his first television exposure, and by 1999 he had his own show called *Predictions with Derek Acorah*, in which he would interact with a studio audience.

I met Derek when I had to step in for the main presenter of the show, and my first impressions of him were entirely favourable. He was a man bursting with energy, both on and off stage and screen. Derek appeared to be an absolute gentleman, seemed humble and, yes, he did apparently have psychic ability. He had a handful of fans who loved him and followed him everywhere, and he would always thank them for coming. He'd put his hands together, practically in a prayer, as he said to them, 'Bless you, bless you, I'm so honoured and grateful to be doing this work.'

There's no disputing that Derek was a breath of fresh air. I remember my mum and grandmother watching Doris Stokes, who was a very famous medium back in the day, and she was a little old lady. Derek, on the other hand, looked like a cross between an American television evangelist and a club entertainer. He had a mullet and an earring, and he wore bright-red clothes and colourful leather shoes. I don't think anyone had ever seen a medium quite like Derek before. Certainly not in this country. If nothing else, he was a consummate showman.

But by the time Karl and I were setting up *Most Haunted* in 2001, Granada Breeze was ailing badly; indeed, the channel would go off air a year later in 2002. And Derek clearly seemed to be aware that its future didn't look good. When Karl and I took him and his wife out for a pizza initially to sound him out about doing *Most Haunted*, he was over the moon; when I went to the bathroom with his wife, Karl told me Derek leaned across the table and took his hand.

'Please give me this opportunity, Karl. I really need it because I'll lose everything if Breeze goes off air.'

As Karl told me afterwards, he felt a little awkward because he was only in his thirties at that time and there was this man in his fifties almost begging him for work because he was facing a possible downturn in his career. I'm not sure if Derek even had any theatre bookings in those days, even with his daytime TV fame; I believe he might only have been playing the pub circuit back then.

Over the next five years, I would have good reason to rue that day, as we shall see. But with our team assembled, we set out to film the pilot of *Most Haunted* in the summer of 2001. Even thinking about that episode now can bring tears to my eyes all these years later. It was our first experience of filming in a haunted house and I'll never forget it as long as I live. It's a bit like thinking back to your first flush of love and remembering how a long relationship began.

I'd seen *American Beauty*, a big Hollywood movie, just before we began filming and we used music from that in the pilot. Even hearing that music now can evoke wonderful memories of filming that first episode.

\* \* \*

Michelham Priory is situated just outside Eastbourne, East Sussex, and the original building was a church, constructed on a moated island in 1229, and transformed into a house 300 years later. We were told the present occupants had experienced lots of unexplained occurrences and that many of the alleged ghosts had been witnessed by members of the public in broad daylight. We were also told the story of how around 20 nurses had visited once, all kitted out with sleeping bags with the idea they'd stay the night. Not one of them had made it to the morning: something had scared them so much that they'd all fled.

Chris Tuckett made us very welcome and proved to be a natural in front of a TV camera as he detailed all the things that had happened to him since he'd moved in. Everything he'd experienced – from the sound of a woman crying and furniture moving by itself, to sudden violent gusts of wind like mini tornados that whooshed around the house – had made him a firm believer in the resident ghosts. He'd lived there for a couple of years, I think, and he admitted that things were so active during his first two weeks of being there he'd even seriously considered leaving. Chris said that, at one point, something was happening to him every single night.

The priory itself is a beautiful building, most of it very Tudor-looking, but I was very nervous when we started. In fact, when I look back at that first location, I think I was more petrified than I'd ever been in my life up until then, mainly because I'd never done anything like that before. Even when we arrived in the daytime I felt unsettled. We based ourselves in a barn, where we ate our dinner, before starting the investigation in the priory itself. I think I lost weight within that walk across because I was shaking so much, even though it was a hot summer night.

I'd heard all the ghost stories and I found the atmosphere in the gothic undercroft particularly unsettling. I was told that a BBC crew had problems there when they were filming a drama some years before us. They would lock the door carefully each night on completion of filming only to return each morning and find all the wigs had been scattered around. We moved from there to the dining room, which is lovely to look at but didn't feel comfortable at all; I thought it oppressive.

During our walkabout, Derek apparently contacted several spirits from different timelines through his supposedly Ethiopian spirit guide Sam. Derek told us that his first name was 'Masumai', which if you spell it backwards is almost 'I am Sam'. Make of that what you will, though much of what he came up with on this occasion at least was verifiable.

Physical activity included a door slamming in front of me and I felt a pinch on my bottom. Derek attributed the latter to the spirit of a little girl he'd picked up who'd lived in fear of a depraved earl and who hid her dollies in a chest down a secret stairway that was discovered only centuries later.

It was the first time I was physically touched during an investigation and I knew it wasn't a muscle spasm or a member of the crew. It wouldn't be the last time I'd be touched, either. And not every time would be quite so playful or gentle.

That seemed to trigger more happenings. We were using EMF meters, which measure the electromagnetic fields in an area and which are often used to detect energy in paranormal investigations. The meters we were using went into overdrive at certain spots, even though they were nowhere near any cables or other source of electricity. Most members of the investigation team saw strange, unexplained lights. And our lighting cameraman, Ian French, was almost pulled down a hatch leading down to the once-secret stairway; this was accompanied by a woman's laugh, which we all heard.

Most bizarre of all was what happened to Karl and my brother Rick, who was working as a camera assistant on the pilot with us.

Karl called out for us all to come and join them in another room they were investigating. This was the first time we'd separated into small groups during an investigation and it's something we've done ever since. Sometimes, one of us will even go it alone and do a solo investigation.

When we got there, he explained what happened when they were sitting at opposite ends of a table by the fireplace.

'Rick felt a tingling,' Karl said, trying to get his head round what he'd just seen. 'I looked over the fireplace and I said to him very softly "Turn your head to the right slowly." He did and he just said, "Oh my God!" I knew then he could see what I could see. It was a pair of legs. Nothing else. Just legs.'

As Rick confirmed what Karl had told us, they both agreed that the figure they'd seen was either wearing a cloak or a coat, which might explain why they only saw the legs. But neither of them was in any doubt about what they'd witnessed.

Our night at Michelham Priory was very eventful and mystifying but we couldn't really assess how impressive it was objectively because, to be honest, we really didn't know what we expected to capture. In our minds, I suppose we were hoping to film the full manifestation of a ghost or maybe poltergeist activity. None of us was really experienced at that point so we were looking to Derek Acorah and the parapsychologist, who'd been doing it for far longer and were telling us that we might capture orbs on camera or record audible phenomena. So we went in with high expectations of what we'd uncover and were a tad deflated that the investigation didn't deliver quite as much as we'd hoped. Looking back now, I realise that was down to the energy levels in the team. We didn't have the right team in place then. Something I didn't know then is that chemistry and good energy in everyone taking part are so important for successful paranormal investigations.

What we did know was that we needed to get the footage edited professionally to give ourselves any chance of getting a series commissioned. So we went to an edit house in Manchester, only to find it was going to cost thousands to do. We would have to draw on every bit of our savings to get it done.

It was a huge gamble. This wasn't only our futures we were putting on the line but also our children's. We did it because we truly believed in *Most Haunted* and it was almost as though some force was compelling us to push on with making the show.

Even so, the next six months were very stressful. We had a mortgage – and it was a very big mortgage, believe me – and we hadn't got a penny left in the bank. We had two small children; Karl was working as a cameraman; and I was only doing bits and bobs presenting for Granada Breeze. We had to live, like everyone else, but we'd used up all our money. Everything was riding on us selling *Most Haunted* to a broadcaster.

The problem was that everyone was turning us down. The BBC did at least grant us the courtesy of a meeting and they did think the idea for *Most Haunted* was an interesting one. However, they'd had their fingers badly burned with paranormal broadcasting. In 1992, they'd shown a horror mockumentary film called *Ghostwatch* that was presented as a genuine paranormal investigative show with Michael Parkinson, Sarah Greene and Mike Smith. It had been hugely controversial because it was put together as though it was a genuine live broadcast, its supposed authenticity underlined by the fact its presenters were well-known and trusted BBC names. The apparent horrific happenings onscreen led to more than 30,000 complaints to the BBC and may even have led to the suicide of a vulnerable young man just five days after it was broadcast. The show is still banned from being shown on any BBC channel, although it is available online.

Other broadcasters just didn't want to know. ITV said they didn't broadcast paranormal shows, though they'd enjoyed huge success and ratings with *Arthur C. Clarke's Mysterious World* in the early eighties. We even approached Granada Television with the offer of making *Most Haunted* as a co-production, but again we were rejected.

The worst refusal came from a broadcaster who told us we were unprofessional for even thinking of making a show about ghosts.

We endured month after month of rejection and it was looking like *Most Haunted* would never be broadcast. We'd sunk every penny we had into this thing and now we were starting to panic because we weren't sure if we could even pay the mortgage.

Making that pilot was threatening to ruin us.

Then Karl did some work for Meridian TV at the Maidstone Studios in Kent. One of his mates was working there as a producer and Karl told him about the problems we were having in getting anyone to commission *Most Haunted*.

'I just don't know what's wrong with this bloody pilot,' Karl lamented. 'We've tried everything we can think of but we just can't sell it.'

'Why don't you go and speak to Arch Dyson?' his friend advised. 'He'll take a look at it and if he doesn't like it, he'll tell you exactly what the problem with it is.'

Arch Dyson was the vice president of Flextech, which owned several channels, and he'd been in TV for years. It was easy for Karl to make an appointment to see him and he took along our *Most Haunted* pilot on a VHS tape.

Karl and I knew this was probably our final throw of the dice.

'Okay, let's take a look at it, then,' Arch said. He took the tape from Karl and slipped it into his VHS player.

Karl admits he was very nervous as Arch watched our show. Arch is a great British bulldog of a man and very supportive of talent. But, of course, this situation was so intimidating for Karl. It was a bit like taking your homework to be marked by the headmaster.

Arch watched the whole pilot without saying a word. Then he took the tape out, still without speaking, put it on his desk and drummed his fingers on the casing, deep in thought.

Finally, he spoke. 'Do you know what, I'm going to take this,' he said. 'One of our channels, Living TV, is failing dismally. This might, just might, be crazy enough to save it. I'll commission sixteen of them to start with.'

I'll never forget what I was doing when Karl called to tell me the news. Like countless other mums of small children up and down the land, a lot of my day was spent picking Lego off the floor. I was looking under chairs and in corners for stray pieces as usual when the phone went. When Karl told me that Living TV had agreed to take the show, I dropped to my knees in joy and relief. Unfortunately I accidentally knelt on a piece of Lego – any parent who's done the same will understand the pain. So I greeted our good news with a mixture of absolute delight and utter agony.

I'd like to be able to say that the title *Most Haunted* came to us in a flash of inspiration, but actually it was created when Karl and I were in a meeting room with the executives at Living TV. We were playing around with possible titles and we remembered there was a show running at the time called *America's Most Wanted*. Karl and I said, 'What about something like *Most Haunted*?' Everyone said 'Yeah, that's it', and so that's what it was called.

The show was first seen on Living TV in May 2002, and without Arch Dyson, there would have been no *Most Haunted*. Sometime later, he came to work for us to produce our *Most Haunted Live* shows and I have nothing but great memories of working with him.

\* \* \*

Looking back now, the whole birth of *Most Haunted* was weird. I've spoken to a lot of musicians, authors, screenwriters and artists over the years, and read interviews with hundreds more. Many of them say that an idea came to them in a dream and I've become convinced that often it's the other side nudging people to do creative things.

I'm a huge fan of The Beatles and I have always been struck by something Paul McCartney said about one of their final and most cherished songs. He was having a bad patch; Brian Epstein had died in 1967 and Paul was going through all the problems with John Lennon and the looming acrimonious break-up of the band. One night, he says his mother Mary – who'd died when he was just 14 – came to him in a dream and said to him, 'Let it be.' That's what the song was called and the first line of the lyrics he wrote was 'When I find myself in times of trouble, Mother Mary comes to me.'

I find that so moving and fascinating. In a very different sense, that was how Karl and I felt when we were devising *Most Haunted*. I know how the initial idea came about but where did the rest of it come from? Why did we feel compelled to press ahead with this project, which was unprecedented in broadcasting and without any guarantee of success? Yet neither of us could stop thinking about the show from the moment we first thought it and I firmly believe that was the other side urging us to do this thing we were meant to do.

We've been to Michelham Priory three times over the years for *Most Haunted*, including for our one-hundredth edition. But whenever I think back to that first visit, the hairs stand up on the back of my neck because I remember the absolute hunger Karl and I felt to go and make that pilot.

Even so, while we truly believed in *Most Haunted* from the outset, we could have no idea just how big it was going to be.

Or the incredible journey it was about to take us on.

## Chapter 4

# BEYOND THE FINAL CURTAIN

*A*CCORDING TO THEATRICAL FOLKLORE it's incredibly lucky to have a resident ghost, so we knew theatres would be a staple of *Most Haunted* investigations right from the very start. To this day, they've often proved to be the most active locations we investigate.

We've visited many allegedly haunted theatres over the years, everywhere from the most celebrated playhouses in the realm to the splendid end-of-pier theatres in Blackpool and Cromer. We followed in the footsteps of Charlie Chaplin and Stan Laurel when we investigated the Oldham Coliseum, although neither of them is numbered among its many reported hauntings; ghosts that have now been abandoned after the Coliseum, once the pride of its community, closed in 2023 because of council spending cuts.

We have also investigated the Royal Exchange Theatre right in the heart of Manchester. That boasts a captivating history as the theatre was established within what was once a huge Victorian trading hall. It survived German bombs in the Second World War and a terrorist bomb in 1996, and now stands resilient and proud, with a ghost story seemingly associated with every corner; ghosts that are seen so regularly that people report unexplained things happening almost daily. Ghostly footsteps follow people around and flowers are regularly thrown off their windowsills when the windows aren't open. Oddly, we were told that it's only white flowers that are thrown; the ghosts seem untroubled by coloured flowers.

No murders have been reported in the building but there were two well-documented suicides. One was a trader from when the building was a cotton exchange who threw himself from a balcony after he lost all his money; the other was a young girl who killed herself in Victorian times. The ghosts of both have been seen in and around the theatre, as have other ladies, wearing Victorian clothing, who seem to be waiting patiently for something. An old lady wearing a purple dress has been seen to roam there; the apparition of a young man wearing a dark suit has been seen lounging against a wall; the figure of a glamorous blonde woman is sometimes seen behind a counter; and disembodied faces appear from nowhere.

The Royal Exchange certainly boasts a richness of hauntings and surely it isn't beyond the bounds of possibility that a theatre like that should retain echoes of the events that took place there, which were as violent and dramatic as anything played out on its stage? Anyone who has done a theatre show and walks through the empty auditorium to get to the bar or their car will tell you that you can still feel the energy of the departed audience. In fact, anywhere where there's been a concentrated amount of energy, like prisons, schools and theatres, tends to be more haunted. If it's true that energy cannot be destroyed, as Albert Einstein asserted, then surely we can accept that places where there have been extremes of energy, be it joy, anger or despair, will be more active?

People who work in the theatre are often very superstitious and maybe that's because it can be such a precarious profession. Superstitions are just beliefs that people like to carry on because it makes them feel more secure, but they can get in the way of serious paranormal research as they muddy historical facts. Even so, it's no wonder that actors and people backstage cling to the ghost stories and traditions of the building they're working in because they don't want to break the spell. In fact, the most famous theatrical superstition of all, the one about not mentioning the title of Shakespeare's Scottish play, *Macbeth*, unless you're appearing in it or rehearsing it, stems from the original production, which was supposedly fraught with disaster.

No one wants to tempt that fate.

\* \* \*

The one theatre that will always stick in my memory was the very first one we investigated for *Most Haunted*: the Theatre Royal, Drury Lane, in London. It is said to be the most haunted theatre in the world.

There's been a theatre on the site since 1663, and the present building is the oldest theatre in the world in continuous use. It has a real mixture of alleged hauntings but the most famous is the Man in Grey, who is supposed to be an actor from the eighteenth century. Every actor and producer wants to see the Man in Grey, and not just because they want to see a ghost: he's a good omen who's said to appear at the start of a successful show! There were well-documented sightings of him before the running of several successful shows, including *South Pacific* and *Miss Saigon*. He's reported as wearing eighteenth-century clothing, including a sword, a riding cloak and a tricorne hat over powdered hair. Seen only between the hours of 10am and 6pm, he sits in one seat at the end of the fourth row in the upper circle before walking and disappearing into a wall near the royal box.

In 1939, the entire cast of a musical who were assembled onstage for a press photo saw him in his usual haunt in the upper circle. That was a group of around 70 eyewitnesses all seeing the same apparition at the same time. Surely that can't be dismissed as a mass hallucination?

No one really knows who the Man in Grey was, but many believe he's linked to a skeleton that was found with a dagger in his chest in the 1840s during renovation works, which uncovered a hitherto secret and forgotten room. The skeleton, wearing decaying grey clothing, was buried in the small graveyard that once stood a few hundred feet across the street from the theatre. It's now a little park and children's play area.

Other ghosts are said to include the troubled Dan Leno, a famous late-nineteenth-century pantomime dame who's considered by many to be the grandfather of British comedy. Leno's unseen helping hands are said to guide actors on the stage into better positions and even give them a reassuring pat when they get a laugh. Then there's the rather terrifying head of the pioneering clown from the early 1800s, Joseph Grimaldi, who is reported to appear in dressing-room mirrors. There is also the ghost who apparently tugs your jacket when you're taking a bow and even gooses dancing girls. The great but troubled eighteenth-century actor Charles Macklin, who murdered a fellow actor in the wings by putting his cane through his eye just over a dispute about a wig, is another ghost alleged to haunt the theatre.

There is also said to be a ghost who makes their presence known only by a strange smell of lavender backstage. Some believe it to be a woman and call her the Lavender Lady. Others are convinced it's a man who attaches himself to handsome young chorus boys.

With such a cast of ghostly thespians, it's no wonder the Theatre Royal's haunted reputation has been a magnet for paranormal investigators, and many people have tried to find its ghosts over the years. James Wentworth Day, one of the most famous writers on ghosts, who published several books about apparitions in the 1950s and 1960s, believed he saw the Man in Grey, but as a kind of blueish-grey haze moving across his reported haunt in the upper circle.

Our episode was broadcast in June 2002 and was only the fourth episode of the run. We'd chosen the Theatre Royal because of its reputation as the most haunted theatre in the world, and it turned out to be arguably the most remarkable episode of that initial series if only because of what all of us on the team saw with our own eyes.

Karl and I were still perfecting the formula in that first year, finding out what worked and what didn't. So much has changed between that first series of *Most Haunted* and the show you see today, but the basic format of spending 24 hours at a given location has been pretty much a constant throughout. We had high hopes that this huge cast of ghosts would put in one big performance during our 24 hours there.

They did not disappoint us.

## Chapter 4

When theatres are open, they're full of people and are noisy, lively places filled with music and laughter. But after audiences have left, they're deadly silent. There are no windows and it's very dark. It's like being in a shell, which is a unique atmosphere. Actors need to be heard at the back of the auditorium, and so the acoustics are such that the slightest sound can be amplified. So you must keep your feet on the ground and not attribute every strange sound to the paranormal when you're investigating in one. I was particularly mindful of that when we made our way to Drury Lane because I already had so many fantastical ghost stories in my head.

When I did my walkabout for the first part of the show with Derek and the parapsychologist, I was reminded just what a beautiful auditorium Drury Lane has.

'I love this place,' I said. 'It's what I call a real theatre. It's got such a rich history. When you look at a place like this you can understand why someone wouldn't want to leave it after they were dead.'

I didn't find the atmosphere particularly charged to begin with. Instead, it was strangely sensitive and gentle. While many ghost stories can be frightening or unnerving, the Drury Lane spirits mostly sounded friendly, even helpful to me.

At first, Derek claimed he wasn't picking up any entities and it looked like we might be in for a fruitless night. But as soon as we ventured into the upper circle, where the Man in Grey is reputed to walk, Derek claimed he had contacted the spirit of a man. Within seconds, he was seemingly possessed and was sweating and upset.

This was one of the first times I witnessed one of Derek's alleged possessions and it was both alarming and, I must admit, somewhat compelling. These possessions became more frequent as the series went on and the channel loved them because they were great box office. Derek would act as though he was taken over by another spirit. He might curse or shout; he would sometimes verbally assault one of us and his behaviour would become unpredictable. No one could guess what he would do or say next. In that sense, I can understand why people were fascinated by his possessions.

I wasn't to know then how problematic they were to become by the time of our sixth series.

Once Karl had helped to pull Derek back from his apparent possession by talking to him gently like you might coax a sleepwalker out of a trance, we moved to the stage. A definite chill suddenly engulfed us and seemingly came from nowhere. I then decided we should switch to night-vision cameras. The lights were turned off, leaving the theatre ominously dark and empty.

But I felt certain we were not alone.

The team had split into two groups; I was in one with Karl on camera, the parapsychologist, and my brother Rick, who was still working with us on the show.

As we wandered around the auditorium, Rick, the parapsychologist and I heard the unmistakable sound of chains dragging across the floor. We turned and saw a man covered with chains walk directly behind Karl, who had the camera pointing at us. Almost as soon as we'd seen the man, he vanished and the sound of the chains stopped; you can hear on the soundtrack that the sound doesn't fade, it just stops.

## Chapter 4

Seeing our shocked reactions, Karl asked us what we'd seen.

'You were pointing the camera at us,' I explained. 'And we all saw a man walking from left to right behind you carrying chains. He was a little stout man, probably around five-eight or five-nine, with dark hair and a bit of a tummy.'

I know a ghost with rattling chains sounds almost too corny to be true, especially as nobody at the Theatre Royal had ever heard of this ghost before, but we agreed that's exactly what we'd all witnessed.

But now the little man was nowhere to be seen. Karl looked around the auditorium to see if he could catch the figure we'd described on camera.

'Maybe he's gone upstairs?' I ventured.

Karl raced up the stairs and searched everywhere. There was no sign of the man we'd seen.

'There's no one here but us now,' Karl said.

We've never understood who or what this figure was. Had we seen a ghost – one of the ghostly comedians Dan Leno or Joseph Grimaldi having a little fun at our expense, perhaps – or was there someone else in the building we didn't know about?

I doubt we'll ever know now. But when we spoke to the theatre's stage manager, our description didn't match any living person working there. To my eyes, the figure looked ghostly and couldn't have been a real person at all anyway.

But Drury Lane hadn't finished with us yet.

I held a vigil in the auditorium and felt an unnatural cold draught over my hands and my legs. And then something blew in my ear, which was incredibly freaky. I also heard a faint whistle.

Later, the crew decided to set up a shot of us walking down a corridor. Little did we know there was something waiting for us at the end of it.

For there, halfway up some stairs, was a pair of legs moving on their own, almost dancing a little jig. We could clearly see he was wearing over-the-knee leather boots.

'I saw them!' someone cried out.

'We all bloody saw them!' I said.

And we had. There was no mistaking them. It was just the legs, nothing more. It was the first location where many working on the show saw something that they genuinely considered to be a full manifestation.

To this day, we have no idea who those legs belonged to. However, not long prior to our investigation, a photographer was taking shots of the interior of the theatre and inadvertently took a picture of something odd. We saw the photograph after our visit and I could clearly see the shape of a figure on the right-hand side of one shot. The photographer swears there was no one there when he took the picture and it was the same spot where I and the whole *Most Haunted* team saw the disembodied legs. Was this the same ghost? Again, I doubt we'll ever get the answer to that.

Drury Lane had one more trick up its sleeve before we left. When Karl, Stuart and Rick returned to the dark, empty auditorium to have one last go at catching sight of the Man in Grey, they immediately felt unsettled, with a feeling someone was following them and blasts of cold air continuously hitting them. Then, they heard a noise and found that the very seat in the upper circle which the Man in Grey is reputed to sit in regularly had come down of its own accord and stayed down: all the other seats automatically spring back up when a sitter gets up. But this one was stuck.

The Theatre Royal, Drury Lane, certainly lived up to its haunted reputation and gave us some of the most compelling evidence we unearthed in our first series. We would go on to gather more incredible footage over the next couple of decades. But it was confirmation to Karl and me in the fledgling year of our show that we were right to fight for, and to believe in, *Most Haunted*.

I don't know if any of the ghosts we encountered that night at Drury Lane was the famous Man in Grey. If it was him, he certainly lived up to his long reputation of appearing at the start of a successful show.

\* \* \*

As I say, I've always found theatres slightly eerie and unsettling places to investigate, although they do also take me right back to the acting roots of my career when I joined the Braeside School of Speech and Drama in Marple, in Cheshire, when I was 13. Up until that point I'd attended a state school known as Bramhall High School, where I was always getting into trouble for telling jokes. I was rubbish at everything, until I got the part as one of the Fairies in *A Midsummer Night's Dream*. I loved it. I thought acting was fantastic. Which was fortunate because Mum and Dad were at a loss about what to do with me.

They decided to send me to Braeside School of Speech and Drama only a year later. I've got pictures I took on my own little camera of the other kids at Bramhall waving me off on my last day there. I think they were as excited about me going to drama school as I was.

I often think back to those days; I'd take a bus into Stockport every morning from my house and looked very posh in my uniform, because students had to wear smart blazers with ties and we all wore boaters. I'd meet up with my friend Angela Siddall in Stockport and then we'd take another bus out to Marple and the Braeside School. I have nothing but happy recollections of those daily journeys.

The school itself was essentially a bungalow sitting on top of a hill overlooking Marple and surrounded by countryside. There can't have been more than 25 or 30 kids in the whole school, girls and boys.

Stockport has produced some brilliant actors over the years, like Claire Foy and Sally Lindsay. The one who impressed us the most at Braeside, however, was Joanne Whalley, because she'd studied there just a couple of years before us.

The headmistress at Braeside was a remarkable woman called Mrs Peach. And she looked like a peach, too. She was round and very flamboyant. She wore scarves and floaty dresses, and had all these big jangly beads and lots of rings on her fingers. Mrs Peach was so very proper when she spoke. It was all 'Good morning, girls. Good morning, boys.' She encouraged us all to speak with RP accents – 'received pronunciation', like you always used to hear on the BBC – just like her.

A usual day at Braeside would see us sitting at our desks in the morning doing lessons in what I suppose would now be the national curriculum. There were only a couple of teachers who would cover all the different subjects. One teacher I recall so fondly was Mr Reed, who took us for English. He was such a lovely, inspiring man.

After that, we'd eat, and I used to love those lunches. They were always amazing. My favourite was fish fingers, mashed potatoes and peas. We were allowed coffee afterwards – it was the first time I was properly introduced to coffee – and then we'd go out to play in what was essentially the back garden.

I met three great mates at Braeside: Angela, who I travelled in with every day, Corinne Fallows – who we all believed was going to be the next great female comedian – and Rachel Shepherd. The four of us were as thick as thieves and we always hung out together during break times. Angela has remained my best friend to this day.

After lunch, it was time for drama, speech and movement. Our drama classes would comprise everything from improvisation – which was something we all loved – to singing and meditation.

I'll never forget those meditation sessions. There we'd all be, sitting around in our leotards and staring at a naked flame in the middle of the room, while Mrs Peach wafted around us, scarves flowing and jewellery jangling, just like Madame Arcati in *Blithe Spirit*.

'Now, darlings,' she'd say. 'I want you all to close every hole in your bodies. That means your vaginas as well, girls. And, boys, that also means the ends of your penises.'

You can imagine the effect hearing *that* had on a group of 13-year-olds sitting around in leotards! We'd look at each other, struggling to hold it together.

Sometimes, Braeside students would go down to the village hall to have dance lessons; I'm sure the residents could hear us coming a mile off as our tap shoes clattered on the stone pavements. But we were all so very proud of ourselves. This was the era of *Fame*, the TV series based on the 1980 film about students at New York's famous High School for Performing Arts, and we all thought we were the kids from it. I mean, when we saw those fictional students wearing leg warmers on the telly, we all wanted to wear them too. And we did!

Braeside students also took part in drama festivals and one of the biggest ones, which still runs today, was the Buxton Music, Speech and Drama Festival. I won best drama prize for a piece I did about Lady Jane Grey in the Tower of London. Joanne Whalley had won it a year or so before me, so my name is underneath hers on the trophy. I was dead chuffed about that. I still am, if truth be known. It was very special because it was the first award I ever won.

There was much excitement at Braeside when all the girls were asked to audition for a new children's television series for the BBC. *Seaview*, which was first shown in 1983, was to be a light-hearted comedy drama series about a teenage girl called Sandy Shelton and her younger brother George growing up in their parents' boarding house in Blackpool.

All the girls were all asked to read for the part of Sandy. Because her character had dreams of pop stardom, one part of the audition was a dance routine set to Michael Jackson's 'Beat It'. We also had to sing a song and perform a piece from the script, which we all had to learn by heart.

The auditions were held at the BBC's studios in Manchester in front of the director, Marilyn Fox, the producer, Paul Stone, and the writer, who was called Chris Barlas. So in we all trooped, one after the other, wearing our leotards and leg warmers to recite the script, sing our song by the piano and do our dance routines in front of Marilyn, Paul and Chris sitting behind a big table.

It really did feel like we were in an episode of *Fame*!

After the auditions, we returned to our studies at Braeside and we didn't hear a thing for a few weeks. Then, one day, Mrs Peach called us all into one of the front rooms of the little bungalow of the stage school. She was holding a letter in her hand.

'I have just had a telephone call and a letter from the BBC from Marilyn Fox and Paul Stone,' she announced. 'And it's to inform me that one of *our* girls has been selected to play Sandy in *Seaview.*'

A buzz of excitement ran round the room. It was all the more impressive because girls had been auditioned from stage schools all over the country. We all looked at each other. Who could it be?

'Yvette Fielding!'

I nearly fell on the floor when Mrs Peach read out my name. I couldn't believe I'd got the part.

What an amazing opportunity! And one I truly never expected. I was on cloud nine. But my triumph was short-lived because suddenly not one of my friends wanted to speak to me. I was excluded from my friend group, sent to Coventry because I'd got the part and they hadn't. I was devastated and hurt, particularly because I hadn't immediately walked around saying, *Look at me, aren't I marvellous?*

My friend Angela admits she feels guilty to this day about how they all treated me. I can laugh about it with her now, but it didn't feel funny at the time. Just strange and sad to be rejoicing one minute but suddenly having no mates to share it with. However, it wasn't long before I was whisked off to Blackpool to start filming so I didn't have too much time to dwell on it.

\* \* \*

Filming on location in Blackpool felt so special to me, as the town had always held such a place in my heart. Something keeps drawing me back there to this day, but I can't explain what it is. Maybe I lived there in a previous life.

As a child, we'd drive there in Mum's Morris Marina. I can still recall the thrill I had just staring out of the window and seeing all these bright lights and colours. It was gaudy. It was brash. And it was always fun.

We'd park up and then walk along the promenade and there'd be all these stalls selling multicoloured stuff like dayglo necklaces, sticks of rock and candyfloss. There'd be a bubble-gum machine here and a slot machine there in the push-penny arcades. I thought they were wonderful. I also vividly remember how you almost couldn't walk because of the crowds and how small children were always in danger of getting lost or being crushed.

'Hold my hand! Hold my hand!' my mum would repeat anxiously, as mothers do.

When I got older I was allowed to go to the Pleasure Beach, which I just loved. There were two rides I really liked. One was the Whip, which was like a long circular platform with cars attached.

As the platform rotated, the cars would move in and out, simulating the motion of a whip. The staff would do the old 'Scream if you want to go faster!' routine and we'd all fling our arms in the air and scream. It was fabulous.

The other ride I loved, and which is still there, was the Grand National. That's a classic wooden rollercoaster which opened in 1935 and is now one of only two Möbius loop rollercoasters surviving anywhere in the world. I adore that rickety old wooden thing and it brings back such wonderful memories; the sound it makes and the feel of the wind in my face. The thing I like best about it was that it didn't go upside down, which I hate. When I filmed at the Pleasure Beach for *Blue Peter* years later, I kept asking, 'Can we go on the Grand National?' They couldn't get me off the damned thing. I would have stayed on it all day if I could.

Within days of arriving in Blackpool, the cast and I were assembled for a photoshoot with the local press before filming started. It felt so alien just standing around or posing while they took their photographs. I was still a kid, really. I stood there thinking to myself, 'My God, what is this? What's going on?'

I can't really remember what my first day of filming was like. I know I must have been terribly nervous because I've always suffered with my nerves. I also know that I'd learned the script backwards. Not just my lines, but everyone else's as well. It was just because I wanted to please Marilyn Fox so much. She'd shown great faith in me and I didn't want to let her down.

Marilyn was such a lovely director. She always had a cigarette in her mouth and was very quietly spoken. If she saw you were nervous, she'd have this way about her to make you feel better.

'Just relax,' she'd say. 'It's all gonna be fine.'

She fell in love with the show's writer Chris while we were making *Seaview*. They'd met on the show and eventually got married. I had no idea then that something very similar would happen to me on another show years later.

We always stayed at the Imperial Hotel while we were filming on location in Blackpool and it felt incredibly classy to me. It had a swimming pool and everything. We had tutors, who made sure we did our schoolwork in the daytime, either on the bus if we were on location or in the hotel, and then we'd learn the new scripts every single night. So it was quite full on.

I also had two chaperones while we were filming. One was called Barbara. She was a larger lady who always wore flip-flops. It could be snowing outside, but there would be Barbara slapping along in her flip-flops.

The other chaperone always used to sneak food into a greasy cloth bag. You could smell her coming from a mile away because of the food she'd squirrelled away in that bag. I remember being in the swimming pool at the Imperial Hotel once and she decided to join us. At one point she came up from being under water right in front of me, and I could see she had a hairy chest. I don't mean just a few wisps but proper hair that came right over the top of her swimming costume. I sort of stumbled backwards in surprise at seeing that and I've never forgotten it.

Some of the students from Braeside were asked to appear in an episode because they needed young dancers in a scene where Sandy and George were being taught to do the foxtrot. I was incredibly nervous before they arrived because the last time that I'd seen them none of them was speaking to me.

I needn't have worried because it was now all 'Hi, Yvette! How are you? Lovely to see you!'

Of course, I was really made up and happy that they were talking to me again.

For the second series, all the studio work was done in London. Maggie Ollerenshaw and David Gooderson played my mum and dad in the show, and Aaron Brown was my brother George. Even when I see Maggie and David in other shows today, I call out 'There's my mum! There's my dad!' They were both marvellous and considering they were working with a load of kids (and that David played the scary Davros in *Doctor Who*), they were very kind and incredibly patient.

In the second series, my character Sandy was given a boyfriend, who was played by Mark Jordan. Mark went on to play PC Phil Bellamy in *Heartbeat* on ITV for many years and I really liked him. To tell the truth, I had quite a crush on him when we were filming together because he was such a lovely guy. We had a wedding scene in the show. It was a dream sequence, but with my little 14-year-old infatuation, I thought as I walked down the aisle that it would be wonderful if we were doing it for real. I remember Mark showing me a picture of his girlfriend while we were on the set – a little bit of me died inside.

My character Sandy also got to be the lead singer in a band in the second series and I thought that was the best thing that could have ever happened to me because it's what I'd always wanted to do. Madonna was a big hero and I'd dance in front of the mirror singing into a hairbrush thinking I was her. Mind you, I think all girls did that in the eighties.

So when they made Sandy a singer in the show I was convinced I was going to be a pop star.

I loved the outfit the costume department designed for that story. They took a photograph of me in it and I carried that picture around with me everywhere I went. I was determined to keep it on me, just to remind myself that was what I was going to do, one day. I was going to be in a pop band and I was going to be famous.

When I look back now, I know I was so lucky to get that show at such an early stage in my career. In the end, though, it only ran for two series. I'm not quite sure why it ended so soon as it was popular; when you're a young actor you don't really get told the reasons why. And I probably wouldn't have understood if they had told me.

\* \* \*

I was only 14 when *Seaview* ended and I still had two years left of secondary education. By then, my dad had moved to live in the USA and Mum couldn't afford the drama school fees, so I had to go to a different school to complete my education where, of course, I was ignored again by all the other kids. They must have wondered who I thought I was, having been on the telly, though I eventually won them over and made some good friends.

I was in a band called Idle Hands for a short time when I was 15 but when I got onstage with them, I was so embarrassed that I had to hide behind a speaker! Still, my son Will has enjoyed great success in America with his musical career, so musical talent is obviously in the genes somewhere.

I did a couple of other acting jobs around this time. I was in an episode of *Juliet Bravo*, in which I was held captive in a house with my mother, who was played by Anna Cropper. But I hardly had anything to do in that. And I did an episode of a Channel 4 series called *Let's Parlez Franglais* in 1984, which was a comedy show based on a series of books by Miles Kington. It was all performed in broken French so unsurprisingly it didn't go to a second series. Rosemary Leach played my mother in that and she was very kind. But the actor who played my father, Peter Jeffrey, was vile. He didn't like children or young actors, so he just didn't want to know me. He was incredibly rude and wouldn't even speak to me.

There was no behaviour like that on *Seaview*. I just remember it as being one big happy family.

In the years after I finished filming *Seaview* I found it strange how little I remembered about the experience. In fact, I remember very little about making the first series. It's only in adulthood that I've come to understand the reason was because my mum and dad were going through a divorce at the time. I think that subconsciously I was so wrapped up in the emotions of everything that was going on at home that my memory, for some bizarre reason, was blocking out all the *Seaview* memories.

I recently returned to Blackpool with my friend Ange from drama school and did briefly entertain the idea of us going on the Grand National again for old times' sake. I then thought better of it: it wasn't such a good idea for a woman of my age!

That recent visit made me rather sad. It was obvious to me just how much Blackpool has decayed, even though the council and the locals are clearly doing everything they can to reverse the decline. It was July when we went, and years ago it would have been heaving with holidaymakers in the height of the season. Now it felt like a ghost town, if you'll forgive the pun. It had changed so much. In my head, I still like to think of Blackpool as being lively and electric. All bells and whistles with everything kicking off. There was no place like it on earth once but it's not like that now. I just hope the town can find some way to pick itself up again and thrive like it did when I was a kid.

Sadly, my recent return to Blackpool wasn't the only time that I'd been disappointed by the activity in the town. It proved to be so much less than what I was hoping for when I visited with the *Most Haunted* team in 2002 as well.

## Chapter 5

---

# HAUNTING
# TRUTHS

*O*NE OF THE MOST FASCINATING ASPECTS of being a paranormal investigator is just how varied the hauntings we've seen have been. They've taught me that ghosts come in all shapes and sizes. We've encountered pockets of pure energy that seem not to be human at all; poltergeists that are sometimes violent, other times playful, but always noisy and disruptive; apparitions that don't interact or are even unaware of their surroundings and seem instead to be a recording or an imprint on the atmosphere of something that happened many years ago.

But no matter how much we prepare, sometimes ghosts don't appear to us at all.

The first and most sobering lesson we were taught regarding the paranormal not always delivering was in Blackpool during *Most Haunted*'s first series in 2002. I was really looking forward to filming there, having had such a connection to the town as a child. And on paper the investigation promised so much. There were plenty of compelling accounts from credible witnesses about spirit children who are very active in the gift shop. And the Ghost Train was even supposed to be the home for a real ghost called Cloggy; a former employee of the park who wore clogs in life and now announces his presence by the sound of them following people around inside the Ghost Train ride where he used to work.

The most unsettling story we'd heard was told to us by the operations manager, Keith Allan, who regularly tested most rides. Keith visited the park as a child and had never forgotten the feeling of the strings that hung down on the Ghost Train in the dark that were designed to make it feel like unseen hands were caressing your face.

Now grown up and working at the Pleasure Beach, Keith decided to walk the length of the track in the dark on his own when the season had ended. He told us that when he reached the area where he remembered the strings hanging, he could feel them wrapping around his neck and tugging at his face. It wasn't until the next day that he was told the strings had been removed a week earlier ...

Hearing a story like that made me hopeful we'd catch a lot of activity. In the event, though, the night was very quiet.

I believed I saw the shadow of someone fleetingly in the gift shop. Some of us thought we could hear a young girl's faint laughter. A couple of us heard unexplained indistinct footsteps following us in the Ghost Train. There were one or two cold spots. And I felt something tap me on the head. That was all.

That location demonstrated one of the dilemmas Karl and I have come up against time and again throughout the history of *Most Haunted*. If a lot of activity happens during an investigation, we often face accusations that we're making it up. If very little happens, people say the show is boring. That used to upset me in the beginning but now I just shrug: you can't win either way.

When we encounter a location where it's all kicking off, we must condense it into a show and obviously want to include the best bits. We can't do that when nothing at all happens. Who wants to watch a paranormal investigator sitting in a room asking, 'Is anyone there?' So we have 78 completed episodes of *Most Haunted* sitting on a shelf that have never been shown anywhere. They are just too boring to watch, like a dinner party where no food is served and no one speaks.

Fortunately, as this episode was released in the first series of *Most Haunted*, we only had 30 minutes to fill. The 16 episodes of the first run replicated everything that Living had liked about the half-hour pilot, including its length. I think it's fair to say that none of us really had any thoughts about the show going on beyond the episodes that had been commissioned – so when we finished filming series one we honestly believed that was our little ghost adventure done and dusted. We were very proud of what we'd achieved when it was broadcast in the summer of 2002, but we were even more delighted and amazed when Living contacted us to reveal *Most Haunted* had given them their highest ratings in the history of the channel. Everyone loved the show but there was one general complaint: 30-minute episodes were just too short.

It was mutually agreed we should make a 60-minute episode as a tester to see how that worked. We made that at Levens Hall in Cumbria and when the channel viewed it, they were delighted and immediately asked for a second series, this time with the episodes at an hour each.

It felt like a dream. It was so exciting and such a vindication of the idea Karl and I'd had. But it also had other implications.

Making a single run of episodes was one thing, but now we were facing a much bigger commitment to the show. I was worried about my children, William and Mary. The family rallied round to help – Karl's mum came up from Guildford, and I had my mum stepping in when we needed her – but I still felt an enormous sense of guilt whenever I went away filming for the night.

Despite all the help the family gave, for which I'll always be grateful, I used to exhaust myself because I'd always rush home to be a proper mum to pick the children up from school and this and that. At the same time, there were scripts to write, locations to recce and meetings with the channel, who couldn't believe their luck at suddenly having this hugely successful show on their hands.

It was a wonderful time, but also very stressful and tiring. And of course because our company Antix made *Most Haunted*, we were also responsible for hiring crew and ensuring their welfare. There's always a turnover of crew on any long-running show but *Most Haunted* is a show unlike any other to work on. Between our first and second series some of the crew had to leave because of other work commitments, but others left simply because they were too terrified to go on.

The most important lesson the second series taught me was how imperative it was for us to get the balance of the investigation team right. Egos get in the way of investigations, and if the team gels we get more activity. I feel that was a bit of problem in the first series. It's one of the reasons we've really scaled back the size of the investigation team since those early days. We're now a core of great mates who love and respect each other, and we get better activity for it.

The show has evolved continuously ever since that first series, and we've constantly strived to keep it fresh and moving forward; thinking of new experiments and ways to do things. But one thing stays constant: the only star is the show itself.

We didn't really know what we were doing at first but with more experience came a growing confidence. As filming progressed and we went on to make more series, I became less frightened by the paranormal and more fascinated by it. That said, I still have anxiety every time I put my foot through the door of a haunted location. That frisson of fear is still there. I suppose that's what keeps driving me.

We have made contact with so many ghosts across the years we've made our show, and we have found the reasons behind why they linger to vary enormously. We've contacted entities who did awful things to people in life and have done horrible things to the investigation team; ghosts who I believe linger in fear. People may like to think there's no hell and even dismiss the possibility of an afterlife, but I believe there's a fundamental fear in most people's minds that they might go to a darker place if they've committed murder or done something horrific. That was even more true in the past when the belief in heaven and hell was perhaps more entrenched. So I think these spirits stay around because they're scared of moving on. They refuse to go anywhere in case something might await them.

Of course, if someone was evil or nasty in life, they're not going to linger when they're dead just to have some gentle fun; they don't change after they die. These spirits are often the ones that we find trying to hurt others. Many of them continue to wreak havoc in the old castles or prisons we've investigated. We encountered one violent poltergeist at Oxford Castle and Prison who was extremely angry. He was a monk from centuries ago who'd been an awful man in life and whose rage and energy remained in the crypt. When we're dealing with a spirit like this, Karl and the other lads on the team deliberately provoke them to get a reaction we can catch on camera. They treat them with the same contempt in death as they would do in life. Sometimes insulting the spirits, challenging them to attack us. It really gets the activity going. We were pelted with objects by the monk and he made terrifying sounds, which we caught on camera. It was scary but, admittedly, provided wonderful evidence.

Not all the entities who linger are negative, however. Not even some of those who were convicted of murder. The spirit of George Riley comes through every time we investigate Shrewsbury Prison. He was just 21 years old when he became the last man to be hanged at the prison for murder in 1961. It was felt by many at the time and subsequently to have been a terrible miscarriage of justice or, at the very least, an unsafe conviction.

Every time we go into the executioner's room, George makes us aware that he's there. The first time we contacted him through the Ouija board, I asked, 'Were you innocent?'

'Yes,' he spelled out.

'Do you know who committed the crime?' I asked.

'Yes,' again.

'Are you happy?'

'Yes.'

'What are you doing here, then?'

He told us he's waiting for the real murderer to pass over.

We returned to Shrewsbury Prison very recently for a *Most Haunted Experience* and George came through with his knocks again, even throwing an old coin at us, but not violently or with any intent to hurt. This time I asked if he was waiting for the real murderer to come over because he wanted revenge.

When George said no, I guessed what his real motive might be.

'I've got the feeling you're waiting to tell him it's all right and he's not going to a dark place.'

George's knocks affirmed this.

'So you're not angry with him? You don't hold any grudges?'

George again confirmed this.

Not all spirits linger with a message. Sometimes a spirit might just decide to stay for no reason. The infamous Enfield poltergeist was a typical example of this. The poor old man who died there wasn't malevolent; he just decided to hang around and cause a bit of havoc and mischief for the people who came after him.

Of course, we don't just visit the violent ghosts at castles or prisons; one thing Karl and I were very keen on right from the start was to investigate a variety of different locations, not just the usual places associated with hauntings. Over time, we've found that audiences actually respond to and are more frightened by the more prosaic hauntings in bog-standard houses and factories – I think it's because they're sitting there saying, 'That could be our house. That could be our workplace. It could be happening to us.' But for me, the more unusual the location is, the more I love it. We've investigated everything from police stations to the *Queen Mary* ocean liner in Long Beach, California. We even filmed one episode at the Ledge Lighthouse in Connecticut. That was on an island in the middle of the sea that could only be reached by boat. Once the boat had gone, you were stuffed and if you wanted to go to the toilet, all you could use was a plastic bag. I came over all terribly British and looked away whenever I saw someone reaching for a bag, but as one of the American crew members put it so well:

'What else am I supposed to do, Yvette? Hang my ass over the edge?'

\* \* \*

It might sound strange to think ghosts can change locations or follow people around but, in my experience, it isn't uncommon. Some of the best footage we ever recorded was at Corvin Castle in Transylvania, where we were based for a *Most Haunted Live*. It was daytime and there was a lot of setting up with cameras and cables. There were still tourists walking around and one of our guys was panning around, making sure everything was working. He captured the image of a white figure rising from the floor, following a young woman, and then bleeding into her body. I find that fascinating to watch and while I never get the sense that the spirit is particularly evil or demonic, it does suggest that ghosts can follow you home. When I think about that it sometimes scares the living crap out of me. It's one of the reasons why, of all the ghosts I've investigated, it's these that have unsettled me most.

Recently, Karl and I were asked privately by a woman in Manchester to investigate a haunting in her house.

When we got there, we found it was a normal, three-bedroomed modern house on a housing estate. We didn't know the woman as we'd been put in touch by one of her friends. On meeting her, we found she was at a loss to understand what was happening to her.

'I don't know what the hell is going on. I have pots and pans flying from the kitchen into the front room. And there's horrible sounds of growling. There's all sorts kicking off. Can you please help me?'

As soon as Karl and I walked into the house, the banging from the walls either side of the hallway became so loud. We listened to the noise and how it was setting off the dogs barking and we just felt for this poor family having to live with this.

'Oh my God,' the woman cried out. 'What is that banging?'

The sounds seemed to follow the woman's 20-year-old daughter around, and when we mentioned this, we learned that the activity had followed them from their previous house, although it had intensified.

Communicating through the knocks, we contacted the spirit, who explained he'd followed them because he thought the 20-year-old looked like his granddaughter who had passed many years ago. He'd just latched on to her and followed her.

'This isn't your granddaughter,' we told him.

'Yes, it is,' came the reply.

The poor young woman had tears in her eyes and pleaded with him to leave her alone. 'I'm not your granddaughter,' she cried.

It was a huge relief to her when the spirit was finally persuaded to leave her alone.

But perhaps the most shocking time that Karl and I have seen a ghost follow someone happened directly to me. I was live on air during a *Most Haunted* investigation of the abandoned Aldwych tube station on the London Underground, which we'd first investigated in series one.

I loved that first episode; we decided to dress in 1940s Army uniform because Aldwych Underground station, which had closed in 1994, had been used as an air-raid shelter during the Second World War. Wearing period dress in this episode was one of the very first experiments we ever did on *Most Haunted*; some paranormal experts believe that surrounding yourself with costumes and artefacts of a particular period can induce time to replay. Certainly there are reports of heightened activity where people do historical reenactments in historic places, and we experienced some chilling activity this night too.

I was very frightened in that desolate station and not only because of the rats. It was dark, cold and very, very quiet. We were also far underground in the most dangerous location we'd spent the night in up to that date. Even though there was no electricity, it was dangerous to walk on the rails in the dark. The scuttling of the unseen rats and the natural human irrational fear of the dark added to my sense of trepidation and horror. And then there were the ghost stories. Many eyewitness accounts of paranormal activity had been reported by reliable train crews and passengers alike.

The most-reported ghost was that of a young woman, thought to have been an actress in the theatre on the site that was demolished to make way for the Underground station.

The team was so unsettled that we didn't split up as we did in most other episodes, and instead investigated the location together. The more we ventured into the tunnels, the more nervous I became. I had to fight my imagination from running away with itself.

Then, as we went through a doorway at the end of the first stretch of tunnelling, some of us thought we saw a shadowy figure walking from left to right across the bottom of the second stretch of tunnel. We were stunned and stopped dead in our tracks. Obviously it was hard to be 100 per cent sure in an environment where there was no light apart from the two or three torches the team had, but I was certain I'd seen a figure of about my height: much too big to have been a rat.

The tunnel seemed to stretch forever and we had no idea where it would bring us out. Curiosity pushed us forward until we could go no further: eventually the terror got hold of me, and I suggested we head back. But then something unexpected and totally remarkable happened: the motion detector we'd set up on one of the platforms started bleating. There was no one near it and the red beam of the detector was too high up to be triggered by a rat, nor could it be set off by dust particles, as we later proved.

Even scarier yet, though, was what we encountered when we decided to return to the location six years later. Everything was progressing normally until, at one point in the investigation, Jon Gilbert, our sound guy, whipped his headphones off and said, 'Oh my God.'

'What is it, Jon?' I asked.

'You have got to listen to this. Listen. Listen … !'

I took the headphones from him and could hear a menacing whisper:

'Y … v … e … t … t … e …'

# Chapter 5

Unless you heard it on the show, it's hard to convey just how frightening that one word could sound, especially as it was nothing at all like we'd heard during our first visit. It freaked us all out but, as unsettling as it was, it was also good stuff. We pressed for the spirit to identify itself. There came just another one-word answer:

'Demdike.'

The mere mention of that name left me stunned and gripped by fear. It was a name I thought I'd left behind at Pendle Hill.

Elizabeth Demdike.

I'd been haunted by memories of that terrible night back in 2004, when I'd seen my friends and colleagues assaulted by forces none of us understood but which seemed to have been instigated by Elizabeth Demdike, the only one of the Pendle Witches who freely admitted she was a witch.

I must admit I was completely terrified. How could Elizabeth Demdike be coming through here now on the London Underground, hundreds of miles from where she had lived and died? On the Underground system that wasn't even built until hundreds of years after she'd been condemned?

We had to sleep on the platform that night and I didn't sleep a wink. I was petrified she'd attack me in the middle of the night and try to kill me. Being dark and so far underground, knowing I'd been followed by a negative energy was the stuff of nightmares. I knew what Elizabeth's spirit was capable of. She had haunted not only my nightmares but those of everyone who'd worked on that *Most Haunted Live* event.

Had she been following me ever since that night? Waiting in the shadows and biding her time? It was almost too horrific to contemplate. I started to wonder whether, if this elderly and malevolent spirit could follow me to locations not associated with her in life, she could even follow me home? It was a terrifying prospect because although she never caused me any physical harm, I had seen with my own eyes what she had done to others.

It threw up so many other questions. Would she continue to follow me? Is she doing so now? I have no idea. What I do know is there was no suggestion in Elizabeth's tone that she was looking for a jolly reunion when she came through as an EVP – an electronic voice phenomenon, a vocal sound caught on a recording – on the London Underground. It was horribly threatening.

I wasn't the only member of the team Elizabeth Demdike targeted, but I was the only one she followed and I've often wondered why she chose me rather than, say, Karl or Stuart or anyone else on *Most Haunted*. Maybe it's because I was the woman in charge on the night of the investigation, telling people what to do and where to stand. That's something she just wouldn't have seen when she was alive and perhaps she latched on to that. Who knows?

When we returned to Pendle Hill to investigate for another edition of *Most Haunted*, Elizabeth did come through again and I seemed to anger her at one point. Later, I agreed to being regressed, which was something I found interesting. But I went under too deeply and only Karl seemed able to bring me back.

All I remember about that now is waking up sobbing with Karl next to me but, if you watch the footage, which I just can't bring myself to do any more, you'll see me screaming and crying and thrashing about on the bed in utter fear. Was that Elizabeth's energy punishing me for what happened earlier? I just don't know, but it upset me greatly.

'Please don't put that footage in the show,' I said to Karl. 'I just don't want it in there.'

'But it's what happened,' he argued. 'And it was really interesting.'

'Interesting for you, maybe,' I said. 'Embarrassing for me.'

However, he persuaded me it should be included and, of course, he was right because it's why we do these investigations.

However, I will not watch that episode to this day.

\* \* \*

Elizabeth Demdike might be a tormentor from the spirit world, but long before I'd even thought of *Most Haunted*, I'd attracted another from the material world.

Who would have thought I would endure a year of utter hell simply by joining *Blue Peter*, the show that has been a bastion of respectable BBC children's broadcasting since 1958?

I'd been very lucky in the first 17 years of my life. I'd had a happy childhood, my parents' divorce notwithstanding, and marvellous grandparents whom I adored. While I hadn't exactly excelled at school academically, I recall my schooldays with great fondness. Drama school had been such fun and my first TV series had been blessedly free of any diva-like egos.

*Blue Peter* was about to make me grow up. And fast.

I first auditioned for it in late 1986 or early 1987; Biddy Baxter, who was editor of *Blue Peter*, had seen me in *Seaview* and called me in for a test.

I thought I did a good audition, so I was devastated when I didn't get the job. When I saw Caron Keating, who they gave it to instead, I could see why they'd chosen her because she just looked so beautiful. For a year, I got on with my life and forgot all about *Blue Peter*.

Then I got a call from them to ask if I'd audition again.

'We all thought you were too young last year, which is why we gave the job to Caron,' Biddy told me. 'But I always watched *Seaview* and I still think you've got something. There's a quality we like there. I'd like you to audition again.'

So I went along for another audition and I took my friend Caz with me. I'd met Caz at South Cheshire College, which I'd attended from the age of 16. She was always an outrageous dresser and that day was no exception; she was wearing bright orange woollen tights that had a big seam where the bum is.

I was much more soberly dressed because Mum, in her wisdom, had very clear ideas about how I would get the job this second time around.

'I'm going to make you look like Valerie Singleton,' she promised. In Mum's eyes, Valerie was the epitome of a *Blue Peter* presenter; after all, she'd even gone on a safari with Princess Anne!

Now, I didn't particularly want to look like Valerie Singleton but Mum still insisted on dressing me in a big roll-neck sweater that came down below my hips, a very long skirt, and a pair of leather high-heel boots that you zipped up the side.

'You'll get the job,' Mum said. 'You look just like Val.'

We'd both forgotten something very important, though.

## Chapter 5

Part of the *Blue Peter* audition in those days was always to do a piece to camera on a trampoline, demonstrating how to perform front and back flips with an English gymnastic champion.

And I hadn't brought a leotard.

'Right now, darling, it's time to get into your leotard,' Biddy declared.

I stood there not knowing what to do until Caz offered a solution. 'I'm wearing tights. Why don't you put these on?'

I asked Biddy what I should do.

'Yes,' she said. 'Put your friend's tights on and when it comes to it, just drop your skirt and step out of it, take off your boots and jump onto the trampoline.'

I can't believe now that I did what Biddy said but I dutifully dropped my skirt on camera to reveal these huge orange tights with the biggest red woollen gusset at the front and back you've ever seen. I looked like a Scottish welder had put me in them.

And then I tried to haul myself onto the trampoline.

But could I get onto the damned thing? No, I could not. Instead, I was left with one knee up on the trampoline and one leg on the floor while my orange backside bounced up and down looking like a huge luminous pumpkin on camera.

Maybe that's what stuck in their minds. Or maybe they just felt sorry for me. Either way, bizarrely I got the job.

I knew I was about to make *Blue Peter* history as its youngest ever presenter at the age of 18. What I didn't know was I'd be working for someone who, while not being a ghost, would haunt me for a full year in very different ways.

No sooner had I been hired than I was doing a photoshoot with Mark Curry and Caron Keating at the BBC. I was in a daze, being with these people I only knew off the telly. But then I saw my mum and brother watching on and I knew it was all real.

Then I was on a plane to Russia with Mark and Caron to film the 1987 *Blue Peter* summer expedition. To be honest, I'd never really watched *Blue Peter* as a kid. I was a *Magpie* and *Tiswas* girl. But I knew about the annual *Blue Peter* summer expeditions and I understood the thinking behind starting me out on that year's trip as it would give me the chance to get used to speaking on-camera before I had to do any live presenting in the studio. I'd only ever done acting before that, where all my training had been to ignore the camera; besides my *Blue Peter* auditions, I hadn't done any presenting at all.

Moscow was a grim and forbidding city in the 1980s, and it could be very frightening. At least it was if you were only 18 – I only turned 19 that September – and had rarely been abroad. In fact, I'd only left the UK twice before I took the *Blue Peter* job; once to Spain when I was a child, and then for a beach holiday in Portugal with a friend.

We were flown out by Aeroflot, which was the Russian state airline. Anyone who's ever flown with them will agree that their notoriety is well founded. To put it bluntly, it was the worst experience I've ever had flying. I remember the hostess coming round pushing a plastic trolley with the duty-free offerings, which comprised some cheap beads and dolls. Then they asked if I wanted a drink. I could see it would be served in a plastic cup that bore the teeth marks of the previous people who'd used it but I still said yes because I was convinced that we were going to crash anyway.

I made it to Russia in one piece, though, and began a trip that I have so many conflicting memories of. For instance, I vividly recall going to the Russian equivalent of NASA and speaking live to astronauts onboard the Mir space station. That was such an incredible and beautiful thing to do.

I also remember getting into a lift with Caron at the Hotel Intourist, which was the hotel exclusively for foreign visitors back then. Caron looked fabulous, as she always did. She could throw on a black bin liner and look beautiful, whereas I was wearing a pair of denim jeans with braces and was plastered with badges of places we'd visited in Russia, trying to look trendy. This look was topped off with my awful eighties perm.

The lift went up one floor and stopped, where a small man got in. He was wearing Ray-Bans and the kind of shiny padded jacket that was very in fashion back then. I was chattering away incessantly to Caron – my accent was much more northern back then – but she started to ignore me.

Puzzled, I asked her, 'What's the matter? Why aren't you talking to me?'

Caron just nudged me and started nodding towards this bloke surreptitiously.

Gormless me kept asking in this artless northern voice, 'What? What? Why are you nudging me?'

The small man got out of the lift. When the door had shut Caron turned to me and swore in her lovely Irish accent – she eventually taught me how to swear properly, did Caron – 'What's wrong with you? That was *Tom Cruise*, for Christ's sake!'

I had no idea that was Tom Cruise in the lift with us while I was just being loud, brash me.

That was a definite highlight of the trip.

For the most part, though, I was miserable and often terrified because the Soviet Union was such a dire place to be back then. I felt incredibly lonely much of the time I was there. I'd sit alone in my room sobbing my eyes out and thinking Moscow was horribly bleak and cold.

One night, a man tried to barge his way into my hotel room after following me on the street. He had his foot in the door and kept repeating, 'I want your jeans! I want your denim!' They didn't have any in Russia back then, of course.

To be honest, I don't know how he'd got past the women who used to sit on each floor outside the lifts. They looked like matrons with big, tall chef's hats and white aprons. They all had walkie-talkies and would monitor everyone who was going in and coming out of the lifts. It was awful.

We spent six weeks filming in Russia in total and I hoped that I would get close to Caron during that time, although I must admit that I was a bit scared of her because she was six years older than me and was streetwise, was already known as a journalist in Northern Ireland and her mother was Gloria Hunniford, for goodness' sake!

Initially, though, Caron was very reserved towards me. She wasn't rude or anything like that, just not terribly warm at first. Looking back, I understand now that she was probably just perplexed why this inexperienced, impudent northern kid had been dropped on her by the producers. We did get a little bit friendlier towards the end of those six weeks, though it wasn't until a year later that we became very close.

At first, the only person I had any real affinity with on *Blue Peter* was Mark Curry. I don't know if it was because we were both from the north, or whether he felt sorry for me because I was so young, but he really put me under his wing and looked out for me.

When we got back to the UK, I was told by the BBC that I had to move to London because I'd be doing the live shows there and it would be the best base for all the filming I'd be doing. My mum was sad I was moving out but we were both terribly excited about me joining *Blue Peter*. She also still had my brother to bring up, so she had her hands full at home.

As a temporary solution they put me in the Chiswick House Hotel, where I stayed for a few weeks.

I was left to my own devices there and I hated every single minute. I didn't know anybody, so had no one to talk to, and I didn't even have much clue where I was. I didn't cope with that at all well, mainly because I'd always been so close to my mum and I missed her terribly. This was all in the days before mobile phones, of course, when communicating wasn't as easy as it is now. There was a payphone in the reception area but every time I made a call home I couldn't speak to Mum because I burst into tears after hearing her voice.

I'd never felt loneliness like that before in my life. Not even in Moscow. Looking back, I was far too young and inexperienced. It felt like a solitary time for me. I was scarily independent. On my first day in the hotel the ladies from the *Blue Peter* office took me to the pub and we had a glass of champagne together. Then later, after a photoshoot, the photographer invited me to her flat for lunch because I think she felt sorry for me.

Apart from being the only member of the team in that hotel, the problem was that all the *Blue Peter* team were in their late twenties or early thirties, while I was this awkward 18-year-old kid who had little in common with them. Looking back now, I wish they'd made more of an effort to help or integrate me. But they probably looked at me and thought, *Ah, Yvette's okay.*

I wasn't okay. I was far from okay.

Then came my first live show when the series resumed broadcasting in September 1987.

I was a bag of nerves that day and when the red transmission light went on, I just stared at it like a rabbit caught in headlights. I tried my very best to combat my stress, but I couldn't help it.

That was the start of my year from hell.

And the cause of it was Biddy Baxter.

*       *       *

Biddy had been the editor of *Blue Peter* for 25 years by the time I joined. She was a strong woman with a fearsome reputation who demanded respect. I was frightened of her from the outset, not least because she was the woman who hired me. She was expecting me to be fabulous and I didn't want to disappoint her.

The trouble was that she was making it obvious to me and everyone else right from that first live show that I *was* disappointing her. And that in turn made me start to doubt myself.

# Chapter 5

Many former *Blue Peter* presenters and crew members have written and spoken about how difficult Biddy was to work for. The late John Noakes had a real problem with her. He would often refuse to even discuss her publicly when asked, but on the rare occasions he *did* talk about her, he was scathing about how she treated him and other presenters. He even declined an invitation to appear in a twentieth-anniversary show in 1978 because of Biddy, even though he was one of the all-time great *Blue Peter* presenters, and would only consent to being filmed for a video insert. That speaks volumes.

I don't know if Biddy's treatment of me was worse than it was for anyone else and, as the late Queen observed, recollections can vary. All I can do is relate what happened to me as honestly as I remember it and to be brutally honest about how Biddy made me feel at the time.

There was no autocue on *Blue Peter* when I joined and we had no earpieces. That meant we had to learn the scripts by heart. Studio days were Mondays and Thursdays, and the script for Monday's live show would arrive on the Friday before, giving us a weekend to learn it. But the script for the Thursday live show would only be given to us on the Wednesday, so we only had one night.

Biddy would come down after every dress rehearsal, which we had on the day of transmission, to give me notes on how I could do it better. I'd rush to take these in, but then often she'd come down again about five minutes before transmission and say, 'Darling, I've rewritten it all.'

Then I'd see she'd taken a big red pen and crossed right through something I'd learned by heart. Even something with a lot of factual detail about, say, Henry VIII or Winston Churchill; things that you simply had to get right on-air. It was horrendous as the transmission light came on and I tried to memorise all her last-minute changes. I'd be shaking backstage, wanting to vomit with fear.

If I messed up, I'd get a call the next day.

'Biddy wants to see you in the Beat Room.'

Every *Blue Peter* presenter dreaded being summoned to see Biddy in the Beat Room. I've no idea why it was called that but it was a fearsome place, even if it was really nothing more than a glorified stationery cupboard. Biddy would sit behind a desk, surrounded by cardboard boxes and pipe cleaners, and basically tell you where you'd gone wrong.

Whenever this happened to me, my self-esteem would go down the toilet and I'd end up in tears. And the more it happened, the more nervous I became. So, of course, that meant I started messing up my lines even more. It was a vicious circle.

My spirits were on the floor as the weeks dragged on and I started to hate being on the show. Part of me just wanted to leave in that first year. But another part of me kept saying, 'Keep going. You can do this.'

Mark Curry was marvellous throughout that first year. He was just such a wonderful human being to have on your side. If ever I was worried about something, I could go and tell Mark and he'd say, 'Don't worry about it, darling. It's all right. Come on, let's go through it together.'

If it wasn't for Mark, I don't think I could have coped; I would have just packed my cases and gone home. He was my only beacon of light in that bleak period. I really looked up to him because he was just so experienced. He was the real deal; he'd been in *Bugsy Malone* as a young actor and had done loads of television and theatre work. So down the line professionally. He would do everything that was asked of him, sometimes going above and beyond. But he would never take any crap from anyone. He'd been around too long as a child actor in movies and stage shows to be a pushover, and Biddy knew he'd call her out on anything she said to him that he felt was unfair. He was an incredible ally to have and is a beautiful friend.

Despite his friendship, though, I sometimes felt so lonely that I'd just take myself off to the park with my headphones on and listen to music. I was shutting myself off from my miserable existence and music was the only thing that got me through some days.

After a while, Mark went to Biddy and the producers and told them, 'Look, this can't go on. Yvette's forgetting her lines and Caron and I are having to cover for her. We're the only show on television now that doesn't use autocue. So can we please have it?'

Biddy eventually relented and I was taken to the *John Craven's Newsround* studio where John himself taught me how to use autocue. And there really is an art to it; there's a marker on the side of the screen as the script scrolls down and you must keep your eyes on that level. You can always tell when someone isn't doing it correctly because if they look above or below the line you'll see them reading. The secret is not to show what your eyes are doing.

Autocue saved my life and bolstered my confidence a little. I still learned my scripts off by heart but at least I now had a backup.

But autocue alone couldn't get Biddy off my back.

She'd call me fat and useless to my face for no reason and I'd just sit there sobbing.

Her put-downs were relentless and over time made me a nervous wreck. I was constantly shaking. They call it workplace anxiety nowadays, but it was really abuse. And apart from Mark Curry and my mum, I felt there was no one I could really speak to about it.

I recall the first big item I'd presented alone on the show, in the days before we had autocue. I knew in my heart I'd done it well. I felt very proud of myself and when the show ended, I bounded over to Biddy with a huge grin on my face.

'You could have done that better,' was all she said, coldly.

She gave me a dismissive look and turned away. I felt utterly crushed. Lewis Bronze, who was Biddy's number two on *Blue Peter* at that time and who eventually replaced her, saw what happened. He took my hand and said, 'Yvette, I thought you did a brilliant job. Biddy shouldn't have said that.'

I moved out of the Chiswick House Hotel after spending a few weeks there and the BBC placed me with a family because they believed that would be the best thing for me. It felt weird to move in with strangers, although they were very nice to me, especially as Biddy would ring up at nine o'clock every night to make sure I was in bed.

I really resented that because although I'd been living at home with my mother before I got the *Blue Peter* job, I was totally independent. I'd got my first job, which was as a dental nurse, had my own car and was working weekends at a bar. I was earning my own money, seeing my friends and was free to do my own thing. I went from that to living with a strange family who had to report to Biddy what time I went to bed every night. She would say it was done for my own good, but it felt like I was being spied on because if they told her I didn't get in until 9.20, she'd make a huge issue of it the next day.

I would have been better off staying in Moscow.

I remember arguing with Biddy that if Mark could go home to Leeds after we'd done the Monday show and he had no filming to do until the Thursday edition, why couldn't I do the same thing? Biddy said no, she wouldn't allow that to happen, although I do accept now it might have been because she was trying to help me to settle in.

Things have been written about me in the past suggesting I was always ill on *Blue Peter* and I really need to set the record straight about that. It's certainly true that I did have panic attacks because I was under so much stress. But I was 18, presenting a national institution twice a week on live television and getting no support, just relentless negativity.

On one occasion, Caron and I were filming an item about the longest waterslide in the UK. I suffer from vitiligo, which means I have no melanin or pigmentation in my skin. Caron and I had been filming in and under water all day, and I'd stupidly forgotten to put any cream on. That night, blisters started to break out all over my body.

I was due to be taken to Cornwall the next day to film a piece where I was supposed to be hoisted from one building to another on a rope. When I woke up, those blisters had developed overnight into sores all over my face and body, and even on my scalp. I was in a terrible state.

One of the experienced cameramen took one look at me and said, 'You can't film in that state, Yvette. You can't even travel. You need to be in hospital. You look awful.'

'No, no, I must carry on,' I said. 'It'll be okay.' The truth was, I was so scared of what Biddy would say if I didn't do it. I was terrified of her by this stage.

They took me to Porthleven in Cornwall and I somehow got through filming the piece where I had to be winched across the sea to a lighthouse. When I went back to London, I saw a BBC doctor.

'Oh my God,' he said. 'You've got third-degree burns and you can't work until they've healed.'

But still I felt I had to carry on. So I dragged myself in and did a piece with Percy Thrower in the *Blue Peter* garden. I couldn't move and could only barely speak. I was in a terrible state.

That was the effect Biddy had on you.

Biddy wasn't even beyond using my condition when it suited her. She took me aside one day and said, 'Right, darling, I want you to do a piece to camera about your vitiligo.'

It wouldn't have occurred to her to ask me if I would be comfortable doing it. Or even if I thought it was appropriate. It was just a case of we were doing it, end of.

I really didn't want to do that piece because I was so embarrassed about the whole thing. She had me standing there in the studio, live on-air, lifting my skirt to show the patches on my legs, and then my arms and the rest of it. No producer would order a presenter to do that today, they just wouldn't.

Then again, maybe she was right in that case because afterwards hundreds of letters poured in from young children with skin disorders saying it made them braver about going to school with their eczema or psoriasis.

'If Yvette can do it,' wrote one, 'so can I.'

That was the thing about Biddy. She made my life hell, but editorially she was so very astute.

I can't deny that I took more time off sick than other presenters because, unbeknownst to me and *Blue Peter* at that time, I had an immune disorder known as Graves' disease, which wasn't diagnosed until a couple of years after I left the show. It sounds horrendous, but it's an immune system deficiency that affects the thyroid. It essentially left me with no immune system whatsoever, so I was often ill.

Years later, at the sixtieth-anniversary celebrations for *Blue Peter*, I met up with Lewis Bronze again. Lewis is a lovely man and I always got on so well with him right from the start.

'You know I was always ill,' I said.

'Yes,' he replied.

'Well, there was a good reason.'

When I explained about the Graves' disease, he said: 'Bloody hell, Yvette, I wish we'd known about that back then.'

'Yes,' I said. 'And so do I.'

We managed to have a good laugh about that.

Towards the end of my first year on *Blue Peter*, I was beginning to feel a little more confident because I'd managed to make a couple of friends – Stephanie Lowe and Mandy France. Stephanie later married Phillip Schofield and I was very good friends with her for several years. I started staying nights at Mandy's house and the three of us would go out together, so I was spending less and less time with the family Biddy had placed me with. The three of us were always singing together and at one point we even thought we might form a band.

I was feeling happier. Then I got the dreaded message:

'Biddy wants to see you in the Beat Room.'

'What have I done now?' I wondered as I made my way to her stationery cupboard yet again with my usual trepidation.

Biddy was blunt. 'We want you to live with Bonnie. You've got until the end of the week then we want you to move out of your flat. We've found you somewhere to live, so you just pack your stuff up and we'll give you the address and telephone number of the woman you're moving in with.'

Bonnie was the *Blue Peter* dog. She was owned by the BBC but had been raised by her handler, Leonie Pocock, who was paid a certain amount per month to look after her. Leonie was absolutely against the idea of Bonnie living with me in a strange house.

'She belongs at home with me,' she protested to Biddy. 'I've looked after her since she was a puppy and I'm all she knows.'

Her protestations fell on deaf ears.

I was devastated. As much as I adored Bonnie and have always been an animal lover, I didn't want the responsibility of looking after her: if anything happened to the *Blue Peter* dog, I knew it would be on me. Biddy gave me no choice, though, and I was in tears as I packed all my stuff together, picked up Bonnie and went to Earlsfield in southwest London to live with a stranger. Fortunately, the woman I was sent to live with turned out to be rather wonderful. Rosanne Macmillan was a BBC continuity announcer and she has the most beautiful voice. She made the whole situation better. Some nights we just laughed and laughed. Bonnie didn't like it at Rosanne's, though. She would spend nights shaking and scratching at the door because she wanted to go home to Leonie.

Through it all, I felt I'd been treated appallingly. There was no regard for my feelings, just a complete lack of respect, and what was worse was that I had recently started to feel better. I'd managed to make some friends and my confidence was coming back. But suddenly, I felt useless again. My spirits plummeted and I felt utterly worthless.

So I suppose it was inevitable that Biddy and I would come to blows eventually. A person can only take feeling constantly terrified and made to believe they're useless at work for so long before they snap. Things had already got so bad that my mum called Biddy directly to complain about the way she was treating me.

'I'm doing it for her own good,' Biddy said. 'I'm being hard on her now so she reaches her full potential.'

But Biddy insisting I must live with Bonnie had been the straw to break the camel's back. One day not long after, I finally quit.

An edition of the show had just finished and the studio sets were being derigged. Biddy was talking to Caron and Mark, while I was due to go off filming with Bonnie. I had my packed bag in my left hand and Bonnie's lead in my right.

I suddenly turned to Biddy and said: 'I've had enough. You treat me like shit and you treat this dog like shit.'

I dropped Bonnie's lead, snatched up my bag and walked out. I was shaking as I did it because I was thinking to myself, *Yvette, what have you done?*

But I just couldn't take any more from Biddy. I had tried so hard to please her and it had put me under too much stress. I wasn't prepared to go through it any longer.

That night, I got a phone call. It was Biddy.

'We get the impression you're not terribly happy, darling,' she said. Which was something of an understatement.

'No, I'm not,' I said before starting to cry.

'Well, let's sort this out. Come to the sixth-floor restaurant at the BBC and we'll talk about it.'

When I put the phone down I thought they must know I'm not fat or useless, or else they wouldn't give a toss if I quit.

So I went the next day and Biddy was there with all the heads of the Children's Department and other producers. And now the tone was suddenly 'How can we help you? We love you. You're doing a fabulous job. Don't leave. We want you to stay.'

'I'd chain you to the fence, Yvette, before I'd let you go,' Biddy said.

That was all I needed to hear. The reassurance that I was doing an okay job. Up to that point I'd heard hardly anything positive.

I told them that I would stay. My relationship with Biddy was a little better after that.

That was the culture back then. It's how Rolf Harris and Jimmy Savile got away with what they both did for so long. I even encountered both of those predatory monsters while I was working on *Blue Peter*.

I was in one of the studios when I was about 19 and doing a piece with Rolf Harris. It was about 8pm and there was only one cameraman. We were looking at a greenscreen onto which they would put up pictures from artists like Picasso for us to comment on.

As we talked, I felt him grab my backside. Then his hand just started going round and round. I remember thinking *What on earth is he doing?* I couldn't believe he was fondling me. But this was Rolf Harris, for goodness' sake. A national treasure. He was an OBE. What could I say? Afterwards, he acted as though nothing had happened.

After we finished the shoot, I went back to make-up and wardrobe and said to them, 'You'll never guess what's just happened to me.'

After I told them, I must confess all we did was to fall about laughing.

'What a dirty old man,' I said. But I thought nothing more about it after that. That was a sign of the times, I suppose.

On another occasion, I went onto the *Jim'll Fix It* show because a young girl had sent a request in to have her two favourite *Blue Peter* presenters serve her some food while bouncing on Space Hoppers. Even now my skin crawls when I think of all the vulnerable kids I saw sitting around the vile Jimmy Savile in his big chair as I walked into the studio. Then he took my hand and started stroking it. 'Look into my eyes,' he said. 'And tell me what you're thinking.'

He was grotesque. I just don't understand why the BBC allowed him to get away with that for as long as he did. Just as I don't understand how they allowed Biddy to treat me and the other *Blue Peter* presenters the way she did.

Of course, I'm not putting Biddy in the same category as Rolf Harris or Jimmy Savile. They were both absolute devils in human form, whereas she was just a very tough, and sometimes cruel, boss. But for me it was all part of the culture prevailing in the industry at that time. Providing shows were delivering the ratings, the bosses on all channels didn't give a damn how they achieved it.

I find it hard to imagine the BBC executives didn't have any inkling of what might have been going on behind the scenes, given the public complaints made by previous presenters, most notably John Noakes. But perhaps Biddy terrified them too.

'Oh God, that bloody woman is coming for a meeting,' the BBC executives would say. 'What does she want now?'

Whatever it was that she did want, she would invariably get it. She always got her own way. I've seen some of the biggest divas in showbusiness meekly doing what Biddy told them to do when they appeared on *Blue Peter* because she was so good at manipulating people.

She should have won an award for that.

Bullying is a word that is often bandied about, sometimes too freely, but I've no doubt that's what I suffered in my first year on *Blue Peter*. One of the first things bullies try to do is undermine the confidence of their victims and my confidence was systematically eroded from the day I started on the show.

# Chapter 5

Biddy was a forceful and intimidating woman to work for. She was hard and ruthless but also very shrewd because she'd say the most terrible things in a certain way. She didn't shout and even had a smile on her face when she was saying the most dreadful things to me.

Biddy didn't care about anyone's feelings. She didn't care if you were ill. If you were lying in the street, she would walk over you in her stilettos to get to the *Blue Peter* studio. She put the programme before anything else. It was her child; it was everything to her. But she broke many people's hearts and will in the process. She certainly broke my will. I have no idea what she was like away from the studio; she might have been a beautifully caring person outside; I just don't know. However, I never felt she cared about me.

At the end of my first year on *Blue Peter*, it was announced that Biddy was leaving. I didn't know the circumstances. I was just relieved she was going.

Yet on her last day I felt strangely emotional. This woman, who I never wanted to see again and who I'd hated for making my first year on the show unbearable, took my hand, patted it, and said, 'Dear, lovely Yvette.'

It really was like working with a narcissist or enduring some kind of coercive control. On the very rare occasions she praised me, I felt like a million dollars. On one occasion, I was filmed riding the showjumper Harvey Smith's horse at Olympia to see how high I could get over the jumps.

'That was wonderful, darling,' she said, coming over. 'Well done.'

I could have cried with pride. But that was the thing with her. It was like having a parent who beats and abuses you: you want them to love you and to like you, and when they praise you, it's the most wonderful feeling.

Then I'd be brought crashing back down to Earth.

I firmly believe that if Biddy was working in television today and she did and said the things she did, she would lose her job instantly.

\*  \*  \*

A year after my miserable time in Moscow, it was time for another *Blue Peter* expedition. Biddy had left and Lewis Bronze had taken over as editor, and *Blue Peter* viewers were starting to see a different and much more confident me. This time we'd be travelling to the West Coast of America. It couldn't have been more different to our trip to Russia. Mark, Caron and I just had a huge sense of relief. It was like we'd been set free.

Caron and I chose to share hotel rooms all the time we were there and we just seemed to laugh all the way through the trip. She introduced me to some of her music and I introduced her to some of mine.

'What have you got in your wardrobe?' she'd ask. 'What are you wearing?'

'How about this?' I'd ask, holding something up.

'Oh, no, no, no,' she'd say. 'You can't wear *that*!'

My God, that girl was amazing. She revolutionised my hair and my wardrobe because I had absolutely no idea about fashion. She encouraged me to get rid of my terrible perm and to have my hair cut short. In doing so, she also helped me to have a little more self-confidence.

It had taken us a while to click but when we did, we got on so well and only really lost touch when she moved to Australia.

I loved working with Caron and Mark, and then later with John Leslie after Mark left the show in 1989. It's no secret that John had his problems years after he left *Blue Peter* but I will always defend him.

I've never seen John behave as anything but a true gentleman, not even when he's been besieged by women. One New Year's Eve, when I stayed with him in Edinburgh, women at the party were constantly putting their hands up his kilt and when one drunken woman made a grab too far, he handled it so well.

'Whoa! Whoa! Calm down, sweetheart,' he said, pushing her away. He defused that embarrassment so well.

When John was dating Catherine Zeta-Jones, they came to me for dinner once. Catherine and I had a cigarette sitting by the backdoor and we did the washing up together.

'I love John so much,' she confided in me in that gorgeous Welsh accent. 'I want to have his babies.'

I thought Catherine was delightful and I told John afterwards that I really approved of her. I was so sad when they split up. I was also amazed when she married Michael Douglas in 2000 and became Hollywood royalty.

I had to share a tent with John soon after he started in 1989 when we were filming in Africa for *Blue Peter* and, again, he was never less than a true gent, always leaving the tent whenever I had to get changed. Sometimes I'd wake in the middle of the night wanting a wee but I'd be too scared to venture out in the dark on my own. The toilet facilities were rudimentary to say the least and I'd have to pull my clothes down, exposing my bare behind to the African moon. John would be there, turned away and a hand over his eyes, holding a torch so that I could see what I was doing. He was like a protective brother to me. I've always liked him and I've seen nothing to convince me that I shouldn't.

I stayed at *Blue Peter* for five years in the end, because the four years after Biddy left were such a joy. I suddenly loved my job. I absolutely adored it.

\* \* \*

After I left, I remained friends with my fellow presenters . Caron and I were reunited when she returned briefly to the UK and we did a *Hello!* shoot together in the mid-1990s. We spent a lovely day together. She showed me photographs of her sons and Byron Bay where they were all living, and I showed her photos of my own family. We were two mums, proud of our kids.

It was all very different from the first time we'd been photographed together when it was announced to the media that I was joining *Blue Peter*. The press interest was huge because I was the youngest ever presenter. I turned up at the press shoot for the official photographs of Mark, Caron and myself, and Biddy said to me: 'This is what you're wearing.'

She'd chosen the most hideous clothes for me and I just thought, *Oh God, all my mates at college are going to see this.*

I was used to wearing ripped jeans, boots and biker jackets but Biddy had put me in pink striped leggings. I looked like something out of the *Teletubbies* or a large stick of rock. Coupled with my perm and my awful earrings, it was embarrassing and I was dying inside.

Then George the tortoise peed on my leggings.

While we were doing that photograph, I noticed that Caron had a tattoo on her leg. I'd never seen anything like it before.

'Caron's got a tattoo,' I said to Mum afterwards.

'Well, she must be a wanton woman,' Mum said. Neither of us knew anyone with a tattoo back then.

That *Hello!* shoot was the last time I ever saw Caron. A couple of years later, in 2004, I was working in the office of our production company, Antix, and Karl came in with an ashen face. He'd taken a call from a newspaper to ask, 'How does Yvette feel about Caron Keating's death?'

He knew I'd be devastated and he came to find me immediately. When he told me, I collapsed on the floor with shock because I didn't even know she'd been ill. She'd kept it very quiet. She was only 41.

Her funeral was unbearable. I went with Mark and we did see Biddy Baxter there. I'm not sure she recognised either of us. I couldn't stop crying because Caron was the first friend close to my age who'd died. It felt so much more dreadful somehow.

After Caron's funeral, I didn't see Biddy for many years until I encountered her by chance when I was in a restaurant with Karl. She didn't recognise me at first but when she did, she grabbed my hand and said, 'We never had any problems, did we, Yvette?'

There was so much I could have said in that moment. But I didn't. She was an old lady by this time so what would have been the point? I just gave her a hug instead and said goodbye.

And that was that.

\* \* \*

It may sound strange, but I feel no bitterness towards Biddy now. That first year I spent at *Blue Peter* was an important part of my life. Part of the journey that's made me who I am. If it wasn't for Biddy, I don't think I would have endured in television. She gave me balls of steel. If I could survive Biddy, I could survive anything.

I also can't deny that I learned a lot from Biddy. She taught me how to present a television programme. Little tips about where to stand or how not to look at the camera when a fellow presenter is speaking but to look at them and seem interested. I suppose she was always this formidable mother figure I respected and wanted to please.

No one can take away from Biddy Baxter what she achieved with *Blue Peter*. It was an amazing job, particularly for a woman working in the industry at that time. The real sadness is that she could have made it even better if she'd treated her presenters better. And looking back, what makes my treatment more baffling is that I went out of my way not to cause *Blue Peter* any trouble. I was such a good girl, terrified of putting a foot wrong. I would never have done anything to jeopardize my job.

## Chapter 5

Years later, when I started my own production company with Karl, I really needed those balls of steel Biddy gave me many times over. I've come across many other bullies in television and I've only been able to deal with them because of what I went through with Biddy. If it hadn't been for weathering what she threw at me, would I have been brave enough to do everything I've done?

I seriously doubt it. So, in a weird way, thank you, Biddy.

## Chapter 6

# HERE'S ONE I SCREAMED EARLIER

*V*IEWERS MIGHT BE FORGIVEN for thinking that because we contact dead people, some of whom were murdered or suffered the most horrific pain and sadness, that there isn't much fun to be had making *Most Haunted*. The opposite is true. We've had such fun making the show over the years, particularly when we're on the road.

When we weren't filming, when we were travelling from A to B, or when we were abroad in the US, for example, we'd go out for meals and drinks together.

Sometimes we have such a laugh while we're making the show; we're always giggling and playing pranks on each other. And things sometimes go wrong. We've got so many outtakes of a member of the team accidentally breaking wind, me thinking it's a ghost and then screaming the place down.

I love all that. It goes to the core of what *Most Haunted* is all about. One minute the audience is quivering under a blanket watching the show, the next minute they're howling with laughter. That's the magic ingredient. We're essentially a bunch of pals going on a ghost hunt and what you see is our very real reactions to what we experience.

Occasionally, I've had to be the sensible one if the others start mucking about, especially on the live shows that Paul Ross presented for us, anchoring the various elements in the studio hub in front of the live audience. Just before we went on air and walked down the centre and onto the stage, the boys would start throwing water at each other's crotches so that it looked like they'd wet themselves. They'd be in hysterics, thinking it was the funniest thing ever, but I would become a bit schoolmarmish as I'd already got myself in the zone to start the investigation.

'Come on,' I'd say. 'What are you lot doing? We've got a job to do.'

Karl once gave Paul Ross an obscure word and challenged him to slip it into one of the live broadcasts. That was no problem to Paul and the audience never noticed when he said it. He really is the most brilliant live broadcaster I've ever worked with.

I know this might come across as being a bit childish but such pranks are common in all levels of broadcasting, even serious news reporting. If you're doing, say, a week-long run of seven live episodes, as we sometimes did, you need to find ways to keep spirits and energy levels up because otherwise it becomes too exhausting. Laughter achieves that. It keeps the energy fizzing and strengthens friendships. Funnily enough, the more we bonded as a unit, the better a time we were having together, the more paranormal results we seemed to get.

It's not just practical jokes that make working on *Most Haunted* so enjoyable. The incredible locations we visit are a definite highlight. Being able to wander around places like the

Cabinet War Rooms, the *Queen Mary* or RAF West Raynham is such a privilege, and we've met some real characters associated with them. People with incredible life stories to tell and, yes, even some genuine eccentrics.

I'll never forget being shown around the ancient Chillingham Castle in Northumberland at the start of an investigation by its very distinguished owner, Sir Humphry Wakefield.

'I've heard the castle is very haunted,' I said to him. 'Do you think it is?'

'The castle is wonderfully haunted,' he said proudly. 'We're very happy about that and they're happy with us.'

'So you're not bothered by the supposed ghosts?' I asked.

'They're not "supposed",' he corrected. 'They're all for real. They're very much part of our lives and we're part of theirs. That makes us very happy.'

'When does the castle date back to?' I asked.

'The 1100s, just after the Norman Conquest,' he told me. 'And ever since the 1200s the same family has lived here. So the ghosts know who we are and we know who they are and it all works very well.'

We were accompanied on this walkabout by Sir Humphry's faithful Labrador and I asked if he ever gave any sign of sensing presences.

'He's always seeing things that we don't see,' Sir Humphry said. 'He either goes up to a spot wagging his tail in a friendly manner, or sometimes looks into a corner and growls.'

What a fascinating place that was. And what a truly interesting man.

# Chapter 6

Of course, some of the funniest moments we have had on *Most Haunted* were those that inadvertently happened – with some of Derek Acorah's alleged possessions, especially on the live shows, causing moments of hilarity. The most famous of these was when we went in search of Dick Turpin on Hampstead Heath for *Most Haunted Live* in 2004. All I can remember about that now is that I was asking him questions when he was supposedly taken over by the spirit of a woman called Mary.

'Mary loves Dick,' he said. 'Mary loves Dick.'

I had to cover my face to hide my laughter because we were live on-air, but on he ploughed: 'Just for a moment an energy came in with a great love for Dick.'

That was it. The crew were losing it and in my earpiece I could hear everyone in the broadcast truck dying with laughter. I had to try to keep a straight face but it was so hard when I could hear everyone else laughing their backsides off.

Fortunately, we went into an ad break straight afterwards and I was finally able to let go.

'Oh my God, Derek,' I said. 'That was the funniest thing.'

'What do you mean?' he asked.

It took a while for us to explain it and he was mortified. He never quite escaped 'Mary loves Dick' for the rest of his life. He was even heckled by people shouting it when he entered the *Big Brother* house in 2017 and I've heard that some people have it as a ringtone.

On another live show, this time in Derby, I asked Derek what he could sense as we walked through a property.

'This is strange, Yvie,' he said. 'You're never going to believe this but you know those greys? The aliens?'

'Aliens?'

'Yes. Well, there's one here. And it's haunting this building.'

'Do you mean to tell me there's an alien here?' I qualified, not believing what I was hearing.

'That's what I'm saying.'

'What's that got to do with ghosts?'

'I'm telling you now. This building is haunted by a grey alien.'

'Where is it, then?' I asked.

'He's there! He's behind that door!' Derek said, pointing to a cupboard. 'If you open that door now, you'll see his energy. It's the energy of an alien.'

The camera closed in as I opened this cupboard door slowly. *What the hell?* I thought to myself. At first, I couldn't see anything. Then I looked down and there staring with a big, happy smiley face was a Henry Hoover.

Again, I found myself trying to control my laughter because everyone else was wetting themselves, and the camera was shaking because the operator was laughing so much. As with 'Mary loves Dick', Derek was oblivious to it.

\* \* \*

Things can very easily go wrong, which prove to be hilarious when you're live on TV, of course. Back when I was on *Blue Peter*, I once had to flip a pancake live on air. I'd practised it repeatedly and it had been fine in rehearsals. When it came to doing it live, though, it all went horribly wrong and instead of a lovely golden pancake in the frying pan, I'd somehow created an inedible glutinous mess.

'Toss it!' the gallery were yelling in my ear.

There was precious little in that pan that could be tossed.

'I can't toss it,' I protested, forgetting I was replying to the voices in my earpiece. The audience at home could only hear my voice and they must have been bemused by my repeating 'I can't' seemingly to no one.

I heard Mark laughing off-camera and that set me off. The item descended into disaster.

I couldn't even look at Biddy when we came off air because I guessed she'd be furious with me. I was right: she wouldn't even speak to me.

\* \* \*

*Most Haunted* and *Blue Peter* are a little similar, in that both shows have given me such a sense of camaraderie and the opportunity to go to places and do things I wouldn't have otherwise done. One of the most memorable was meeting Princess Diana in 1992.

*Blue Peter* had launched a design competition in January of that year for the upcoming Expo '92 in Seville. The winner was to be flown to Seville with myself and John, and to meet Princess Diana in the British building at the exhibition.

It was all going to be done live and the plan was that Prince Charles and Princess Diana would walk through the British building and Diana would stop to talk to the competition winner with me standing by them.

As it was live, our editor Lewis Bronze urged me to keep Diana talking as long as I could so they could get as many shots as possible. The men in grey suits from the Palace had other ideas.

Just before we went live, they came over to speak to me.

'You don't talk, unless you are spoken to,' they instructed. 'You don't ask the princess any questions. If you do speak to her because she's asked a question, then you call her ma'am.'

In other words, don't speak to her at all if possible.

I stood with our competition winner – a sweet girl, who was about nine or ten – as Princess Diana made her way towards us. Lewis Bronze's plea that I keep Diana talking for as long as possible was ringing in my ears and I thought, *Right, I don't care what those men in suits said,* so I spoke to her first.

'Hello, ma'am,' I said. 'Are you having a lovely time?'

I then introduced our competition winner and Diana was just lovely with her. We started chatting and Diana said: 'I love *Blue Peter.* William and Harry curl up with me on the sofa and we snuggle while we watch it together.'

I remember thinking that was a lovely thing for her to say. I also recall glancing down at her shoes and noticing she had fake tan on her legs, which had streaked. That was a real surprise to me.

I got a huge pat on the back from Lewis and the production team for keeping her talking for as long as I did. It felt like ages but, in truth, it was probably not more than a minute.

The lasting impression I had from seeing her with Prince Charles was that she was so unhappy. She clearly didn't want to be there and looked like she wanted to burst into tears most of the time. It was only when we spoke to her like a normal person that Diana's eyes seemed to come alive and she was happy just to chat to this little girl and me. It was obvious to me that there was something fundamentally wrong in her life. We all know that

## Chapter 6

Diana was no angel, and it's forgotten now just how sick and tired we all were of the media coverage of her marital woes before she died. Even so, her sudden death in 1997 was such a terrible shock and I feel so sad at how miserable that poor woman clearly was in those final years.

There were many other almost unbelievable assignments on *Blue Peter*. For instance, I still recall the thrill I had when I was perched hundreds of feet above ground right in the centre of the giant steerable telescope dish at Jodrell Bank Observatory in Cheshire. I'd been so excited when I received the call asking whether I'd like to paint it, and even more so when my dad told me that he'd dug the foundations for the telescope. The dish – which is officially called the Lovell Telescope, named after the astronomer Sir Bernard Lovell – doesn't look all that big when you drive past it. But when you're standing underneath it, or when you're on the dish itself, you realise just how massive it really is.

I remember going up the steps, which were within the supporting legs, all the way to the top and walking through a hatch door on to the actual dish. Cheshire is my home and it always looks beautiful to my eyes, but I'd never seen it quite like that before. It was fantastic just to be looking out on such a stunning vista from that height. The houses, cars and roads all looked so tiny, and the people were just like ants.

I was given a roller and started painting the inside of the dish. I really enjoyed doing that. Then the time came to paint the legs on the outside. That meant I had to be put into a harness, get my arms and legs out of a little window at the top of the dish and crawl out backwards to nowhere before abseiling down with a pot of paint on one side of my belt and a paintbrush on the other.

While I'm not scared of heights, I am terrified of falling. I sometimes dream I'm falling from high up, although the dream always stops before I hit the ground. So I was full of trepidation about this. Not as much as the poor cameraman, however.

They needed to capture my reactions for the film. These days, that would have been achieved by using a drone hovering alongside me, but there were no drones in those days and a proper camera-man was required to crawl out on to the other leg to capture what I was doing and saying. This poor man was terrified and he burst into tears as he edged out. He was shaking with fear so much that they had to haul him back in before he could film anything.

I'm not sure how they got the shots of me painting the leg after that, but I do recall there were very few of them when the film was broadcast.

It was an extremely dangerous task and I feel very proud of myself that I made it all the way down successfully that day. When I drive past Jodrell Bank, which I do two or three times a week these days, I always think of that assignment. And occasion-ally I'll say to myself: 'That dish looks a bit dirty. It could do with a lick of paint.'

Some years earlier, John Noakes had climbed Nelson's Column in Trafalgar Square for the show without a safety harness, so I was following a fine tradition.

Things did change in terms of health and safety during the time I was working on the show. Suddenly we always had to have someone from health and safety with us whenever we filmed.

On one occasion we were filming a piece about me canoeing in Wales in winter. Shooting the rapids and that kind of thing. The production team was keen on showing me performing an Eskimo roll, which is where you correct a capsized kayak with your body motion and the paddle. I'd practised this manoeuvre in a swimming pool in London before we went to Wales but I never could manage to do it. I couldn't do it when we got to Wales, either, and it was freezing cold.

'We've got to get this, Yvette,' the director said.

Then the health and safety officer intervened. 'She's been in the water too long,' he told the director and then ordered me out of the kayak.

I felt terrible because the last thing I wanted was to go back to my first year when Biddy Baxter was blaming me for being useless at everything. But there was no arguing with the health and safety guys. If they decided you'd been in the water or the air or whatever for too long, that was it. So out I came.

I only wish they'd been there in my first year when I felt compelled to work with my awful sunburn.

\* \* \*

Another memorable *Blue Peter* assignment came in 1988 with the British Olympic bobsleigh team in Germany.

It started when I got a call from one of our directors, Nick Heathcote. I was still living at Rosanne Macmillan's and I had a phone in my bedroom. There were no mobile phones for us in those days.

'Hi, Yvette,' he said brightly. 'How do you fancy going bobsleighing in Germany?'

'Oh my God,' I said. 'That would be amazing. I can't wait.'

'Great,' he said. 'We leave next week and you're going to be doing it with the British Olympic bobsleigh team.'

I was so excited by this, especially as I loved working with Nick. He had a cigarette in his mouth permanently and was like an older brother whenever we filmed together. But the thing was, in my innocence I thought that bobsleighing was just like tobogganing. I knew what a bobsleigh looked like, of course, but in my head it was something quite gentle that you did on the flat and that it was all over quickly.

I found out soon enough how wrong I was.

It was early evening when we arrived in Germany, but it was already dark as it was winter. I was introduced to Nick Phipps, the captain, and the rest of his GB bobsleigh team. They were all brilliant and, again, just like the biggest, most protective brothers I could have wished for.

Before we went in to dinner, Nick Phipps suggested we go and have a look at the track. We were driven to a point that gave the best vantage point.

In front of me was the biggest mountain you can think of. It looked like a huge Mr Whippy ice cream and the track weaved all the way down from the top to the valley. I was convinced I was going to die the next day.

I turned to Nick Phipps and said, 'You are joking me? I thought it was flat.'

The lads all fell about laughing at that.

## Chapter 6

'You'll be fine,' Nick Phipps assured me. 'We won't let anything happen to you.'

The following day they were going to be doing one of the practice runs for the actual run they would do. I was to be in one of the practice runs.

The first thing we did was to walk the course with Nick Heathcote. If I was scared the previous night, I was doubly so now. The ice walls were huge, maybe 12 feet high, and I could see the marks where the bobsleighs had careered off the course or had crashed. Everyone else thought it was enormous fun and was having a great time. But I felt very vulnerable.

When we got back to the top of the course, I was a bit embarrassed as we all had to put on Lycra one-piece suits. Believe me, those suits leave nothing to the imagination and there was I, this little teenager with her panty line showing, among all these handsome, gorgeous men who were built like brick outhouses. Their muscles were bulging through the suits and you could see what they were all packing for lunch!

Nick Phipps said to me, 'We'll start off with you already sitting in the sleigh because you're so light and the rest of us will jump in when we pick up speed.'

So I'm sitting there when they did the whole 'One ... two ... three ... !' routine and then the light went on and we were away.

At first, it seemed to be going slowly. But then the pace picked up quickly. Suddenly it was going incredibly fast and I was terrified. The G-force was so strong that I couldn't even lift my head to see where we were going. You get thrown around so much in a bobsleigh and end up with a mass of bruises. My body was being tested to the limits and the only thing I could think of to take my mind off what was happening was to sing.

I'd watched a Steve Martin film, *Three Amigos*, the previous night and there's a song in that called 'My Little Buttercup'. In my stupidity I decided to sing it all the way down to the bottom to take my mind off the horror of what was happening.

When it was over, Nick Heathcote decided they needed me to do a second run to get some cut-away shots. I told them there was no way I was doing that again. I was physically shattered and had nearly wet myself halfway through from fright.

Nick came up with a solution. He pulled on a Lycra suit to act as my body double for the second run. The only problem with that is Nick is about six feet tall and almost as much across. So anyone watching that film closely saw me miraculously put on about five stone and grow in height in some shots.

That all seemed fine until the next morning when they came to view the raw footage and suddenly everyone was very cross with me. I couldn't understand why until Nick Heathcote said to me: 'I can't believe you sang "My Little Buttercup" all the way down the mountain. We can't use the soundtrack.'

I was mortified. 'I'm so sorry,' I said. 'I was just so frightened that I didn't think.'

Nick decided that we would have to rerecord the sound. I wasn't sure how without doing the whole run again, which I didn't want to do. But he suggested we could recreate it in another way and led me to the hotel car park. I was dubious, but happy to consider any alternative to my getting back in that bloody bobsleigh.

I got into the front seat of the hire car, with a microphone on. Nick sat directly behind me, and the production PA was in the driving seat. The sound recordist stood outside the car wearing his earphones.

Nick thought we needed to emulate the rattle of the bob-sleigh, so they started shaking and rocking my seat while I'm screaming, 'I think it's turning now! We're turning to the left … !' trying to recapture the scene in my head when I was racing down the mountain.

As it was winter and there was thick snow all around us, the car windows started to steam up very quickly.

A steamed-up car, rocking and shaking, with a woman's screams coming from inside and an incongruous-looking man standing outside with recording equipment was bound to attract attention. And soon we were having to convince the German police that we weren't making a porn film. Fortunately, they found it very funny when we told them what we were doing.

\* \* \*

My favourite of all my assignments for *Blue Peter*, though, was flying the Royal Navy Sea King helicopter in 1990. I'd always been drawn to joining the military from being a little girl: I love the idea of the camaraderie of the forces. The director of this item was Alex Leger, who was another of my favourite directors to work with and remains a friend to this day. We went to Royal Naval Air Station Culdrose in Cornwall so I could train on a simulator first. I found out much later that Karl, who'd worked in an architect's office, had helped design where that simulator was going to be.

I completed all my training on the simulator and then, the following day, I was to fly this Sea King helicopter, weather permitting. I was introduced to all the crew, who were just so patient and supportive with me. I still have the team photograph, which they all signed for me.

I got into all the flying gear, the helmet and gloves and everything, and then I sat in the front cockpit next to the captain. You steer a helicopter with your feet and there's a kind of joystick, which you twist to go up and down. As I settled into position, I started shaking – not with fear but excitement. Obviously, I didn't want to let anyone down or make any silly mistakes, so I was careful not to be overconfident. But I knew I'd done well on the flight simulator and really believed I could pull this off. I couldn't wait to get into the air.

We started the engine and went through all the checks. I spoke with the captain through headphones and I remember just how calm and softly spoken he was. He took us up into the air and to a height of about 100 feet or so. Then he calmly said: 'Yvette, I'd now like you to take over.'

And that was that. I just kept my feet even, put my hand on the stick and then the captain said, 'You have full control.'

'Oh my gosh!' I said, as we weren't allowed to say, 'Oh fuck!' on *Blue Peter*. But I had to say something because it felt so amazing to be in control of such a wonderful, powerful machine.

I flew that helicopter for about 30 minutes. Admittedly, it was in a straight line and I didn't take off or land it. I also knew I had the captain beside me who could take over at any second if he had to. But I still felt a sense of elation that I'd done it when we landed. How many people would get the opportunity to fly a Sea King helicopter if they weren't in the Navy?

The Sea King helicopter might be my favourite *Blue Peter* assignment, but the viewers had other ideas when the *Radio Times* asked them to name the best *Blue Peter* film in a poll to mark the show's sixtieth birthday in 2018. Bizarrely, it was Mark Curry and me on a rollercoaster in Blackpool that came out on top.

That edition of *Blue Peter* was devoted to Blackpool, especially the history, the beach and the fun fair. The Pleasure Beach had recently acquired the Revolution, which was Europe's first fully looping rollercoaster. We'd never seen anything like it in England before, so naturally enough *Blue Peter* decided that Mark and I should ride it.

I was terrified of getting on this bloody thing so Mark kept having to reassure me.

'It'll be fine, Yvette. Let's just get on with it.'

It wasn't fine. It was awful.

I screamed all the way round the track, then it was suggested we do it again – backwards. To make the ride go backwards required a key, which was kept in the control box. I'm not quite sure how I did it now, but I grabbed the key and shoved it down my bra so that no one could have it.

I wasn't being a diva. I never have been. It was all done with lots of laughs and, besides, the director admitted he'd got more than enough footage the first-time round.

More hilarity ensued when we got back to the studio and the editors said that mine was probably the longest scream ever recorded in one breath.

I'm still amazed that sequence was voted the fans' favourite ever moment. To my mind, that honour should go to Lulu the elephant relieving herself live in the studio and John Noakes, Peter Purves and Valerie Singleton trying to maintain order as the handler lost control of her and slipped in what she'd deposited. Now that's a classic.

People seemed to love the screaming, though. Little did I know then that my scream was going to become more famous. I was meant to scream on television. I was born to scream.

That clip of Mark and myself has been viewed many times on YouTube, but I try not to ever watch or hear myself back. I hate it and cringe whenever I do, which sadly happens often when you're having to record a voiceover. It's always like listening to your voice on an answering machine.

The only bits from the *Blue Peter* days that I will watch now are the song and dance extravaganzas we used to do at Christmas. They were fantastic, because the producers would spend quite a chunk of the budget to create the steps and costumes. We had a proper musical director and Cherry Gillespie from Pan's People was our choreographer.

Mark Curry and I once did a whole 'Puttin' on the Ritz' number, complete with a fountain. And there was one year where Mark, Caron and I were in a hot-air balloon visiting different countries. We sang 'The Coffee Song (They've Got an Awful Lot of Coffee in Brazil)' and did 'The Sand Dance' in Egypt.

We used to put so much work into those routines and rehearsed so hard. Sometimes we rehearsed until one in the morning, and then we had to go off filming or into the studio the next day, but we didn't mind that at all because we all just loved it.

That was the thing about *Blue Peter*. One minute you could be flying a Sea King helicopter, the next you were performing a Fred and Ginger tap-dance number. It was a fantastic job.

I'm sometimes asked why I left *Blue Peter* when I did in 1992, particularly as the new team of Diane-Louise Jordan, John Leslie and I had really gelled and were working well together. However, I'd clocked up five years on the show by that stage.

I'd done a lot of filming prior to going straight to Seville for the Expo '92 piece and then I was told immediately I was doing the summer expedition for six weeks in New Zealand on my own because John and Diane weren't available to film. I even had to buy new knickers for that expedition because I didn't have enough time to get home to pack properly.

By this stage I was feeling much more confident about the show and I knew how it all ticked. I'd gone from being a bullied, nervous 18-year-old kid to a strong, confident senior member of the team. Yet I was still very much a presenter as far as the production staff were concerned; I felt that a lot of the show was resting on my shoulders, but even though many of my suggestions for items were taken on board, I was still frustrated that I couldn't contribute more. After five years I felt it was time for me to try something different.

I told John Comerford, who was one of our producers on the New Zealand shoot, that I was thinking of leaving. By the time the gruelling six weeks were up, my mind was made up. I told Lewis Bronze that I wanted to leave as soon as I got back to the UK.

\* \* \*

After I left *Blue Peter*, I considered leaving television altogether and was toying with the idea of either signing up for the military or becoming a teacher.

However, by then I had an agent and before long I heard through them that ITV were doing a new morning children's show on Saturdays and that the producers would like to have a chat with me. I went to meet Vanessa Hill and Ged Allen in Maidstone who introduced me to *What's Up Doc?*, which was to be produced in association with Warner Brothers. Vanessa and Ged explained the format would be two guys and one female presenter, and showed me a mock-up of the set.

The show would include cartoons from Warners' Looney Tunes library, and there'd be phone-in games and lots of music. They asked me if I'd be interested and I said I would be, since we got on like a house on fire. They were so funny, down to earth, had my sense of humour and both smoked like troopers. For ages, I heard nothing back from them and was convinced that I hadn't got the job. But then one day I was at my grandparents' house in Bredbury, just south of Manchester, when I got a call. It was Vanessa, who'd been trying to track me down.

'Congratulations!' she said. 'You've got the job.'

I couldn't believe it. I knew that moving to ITV was a huge thing but it also felt that by leaving *Blue Peter* and going on to something else I was really growing up.

So I said yes.

What was a girl to do? Life had moved on and I had a mortgage to pay and the BBC weren't flooding me with offers after I said I wanted to leave *Blue Peter*. My leaving party ended up being a bleak affair. They knew I'd accepted the ITV job and were annoyed with me, not only for leaving them, but also for joining ITV's new Saturday kids' show. I knew they wouldn't exactly be celebrating my departure, but the atmosphere was so horrible that I didn't enjoy it at all. A few years later, Lewis Bronze and I met for lunch where he apologised for how *Blue Peter* had treated me when I left. I told him I forgave them all, and I meant it. Lewis was such a caring producer to work with. He was exactly what I needed after my first year with Biddy.

In the event, *What's Up Doc?* proved to be pivotal in my career. Not only were Vanessa and Ged two of the most amazing producers I've ever worked with, it was also the transition show between my being purely a children's presenter on *Blue Peter* to presenting for adults, and the first time in my career I'd been allowed to contribute to the writing. I was really made to feel like an integral part of the creative team.

The show had a deliberately chaotic feel to it and was one of the most fun things I've ever done in television. We broadcast live, tapping into the same anarchic and slapstick vibe that *Tiswas* had. I grew up watching *Tiswas*, which had occupied the same Saturday morning slot on ITV for years, a decade or so before *What's Up Doc?*, and I remember my dad roaring with laughter at it. I wasn't quite sure why he was laughing so much but I was just pleased he was enjoying it as much as I was. What I didn't realise was he was laughing at the innuendoes that flew over my head.

*What's Up Doc?* followed that fine tradition and we were always getting into trouble from the Independent Television

Commission – which predated Ofcom in overseeing the standards of independent TV companies – because of how near the knuckle we got.

I presented the show with Andy Crane and Pat Sharp, and we'd have a variety of wonderful Jim Henson puppets to work with. Music was a big part of the show and we helped launch the careers of some of the biggest names in pop. We even had Take That, and both the Minogues – Kylie and Dannii. We were also the first ITV Saturday morning kids' show to beat the BBC for viewing figures. Even by our fourth episode, everyone had turned to us.

The puppets were such great characters. One was Pasty, a cockney earthworm who'd appear from pots or behind the sofa. He'd wear a wristwatch round his neck and another worm, his wife, Mrs Pasty, would ask, 'Have you got the time on you, cock?'

Another character was called Mr Spanky. He had the most hideous, frightening look, with a distorted yellow face and spiky hair. He'd look into the camera and say, 'If you're naughty, Mr Spanky's going to spank you.'

We would put children in cages – which was very reminiscent of *Tiswas*, of course – and have two wolves to eat them. The kids lapped it up. It might not have been a *Blue Peter* badge, but to be eaten live on TV by one of the wolves on *What's Up Doc?* was a real badge of honour, nonetheless.

One of the most memorable characters was called Simon Perry. Simon was an anorak who dressed as a cyclist and who was obsessed with cheese. He brought a cockerel once, stuck it under his arm and asked our celebrity guests if they'd like to stroke his cock.

## Chapter 6

Looking back, I can't believe we got away with what we did. It's no wonder the bosses at ITV were worried Warner Brothers might pull their investment from us. But the kids relished the anarchy, while the parents appreciated the double entendres, and we loved doing it. And because it was done live, there was always that added excitement of unpredictability.

I loved working with Ged and Vanessa because I respected them so much. Ged knew so much about comedy and he taught me a lot about it. In fact, I learned so much from both of them. They were always so pleasant. If they felt I could have done something better, they would never tell me in a horrible way.

I had a little Mini at the time and I used to just love driving up to Maidstone from Surrey, where I was then living, on a Thursday to prepare the next Saturday show. Andy, Pat and I would sit in the production office with Vanessa and Ged, going through the letters the viewers had sent in. Then we'd go through all the ideas for the next show. It wasn't a script as such at this point; we'd just all work on ideas.

We'd then meet up in a village hall first thing on the Friday, by which time a script had been written up, and rehearse for the live show the following day. We were free to ad-lib on air, though, which was refreshing. Inevitably we'd all end up having a drink together afterwards, cast and crew. I was oblivious to a young camera assistant called Karl Beattie working with me at the time – we wouldn't meet until after I'd left a few years later.

For a time, I rented a little a little cottage in Kent with one of the puppeteers, John Ecclestone, to be nearer the studios.

Pops. A true war hero and an inspiration.

Beautiful Grandma Mary, Pops and Tilly the dog.

*Above:* Mum.
What a stunner!
One of my favourite
pictures of her.

*Left:* Me and my
dad, Alan. Look at
my chunky knees!

*Above:* Posing for a competition. My career started early.

*Right:* Me, aged five, looking very smart in my school uniform.

*Left:* Getting ready for school. Got my lunchbox, got my Dobermann.

With best friend Ange. On the left, aged 14 with our pearls and perms at the ready! On the right, in Oxford on one of our many recent adventures.

*Above:* Having a rest between takes on Blackpool beach filming *Seaview*.

*Right:* Me, Mark Curry and Caron Keating in front of Saint Basil's Cathedral, Russia, during the 1987 *Blue Peter* summer expedition.

The red bow! What was I thinking? Even Bonnie didn't like it.

Baldrick (Tony Robinson) from *Blackadder* came to visit the *Blue Peter* studio, where pandemonium ensued. We often had fun on set.

*Left:* Overjoyed and thrilled that I had just flown a Sea King helicopter. A moment from 1990, captured forever.

*Below:* Filming for the *Blue Peter* summer expedition in New Zealand, 1992. I loved this trip, but I was battling with myself about whether to leave the show or not.

A crew picture from *What's up Doc?*. There's me, centre right.

Filming for *What's Up Doc?* in LA. Interviewing Mr David Hasselhoff. Better legs than me!

Me and Karl in 1998. One of our earliest photos together. We decided to buy our first pets: some plastic battery-operated fish. They died!

Our wedding day, 1999. What am I whispering to my husband?

*Above:* Me cooking dinner in our first home in Cheadle Hulme, Cheshire. The house that had to be blessed.

*Right:* Cuddling my two adorable, beautiful children, William and Mary.

*Above:* Me and Karl at the start of *Most Haunted*. Little did we know what was to come.

*Right:* Trying to look spooky, coming across more constipated.

*Above:* Filming a *Most Haunted* opening piece, with yours truly driving a tank.

*Left:* Me and Paul O'Grady in Venice, boarding the boat that would take us into haunted waters.

*Right:* The burns on Karl's forearms after a terrifying night at 30 East Drive.

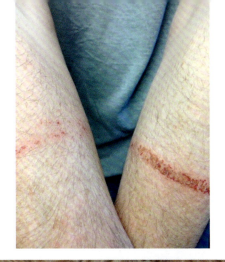

*Below:* Getting blessed in Las Vegas. Who doesn't want to get married by Elvis?!

*Above:* The *Most Haunted* team today. Top left: Stuart Torevell, Karl, Glen Hunt. Bottom Left: Darren Hutchinson, me and Gregg Smith.

*Left:* Hosting the *Most Haunted* stage show. What an absolute joy!

Looking for spooks at MI6 with my wonderful friend and co-writer, Martin Sterling.

Mary, Karl and me. The three musketeers.

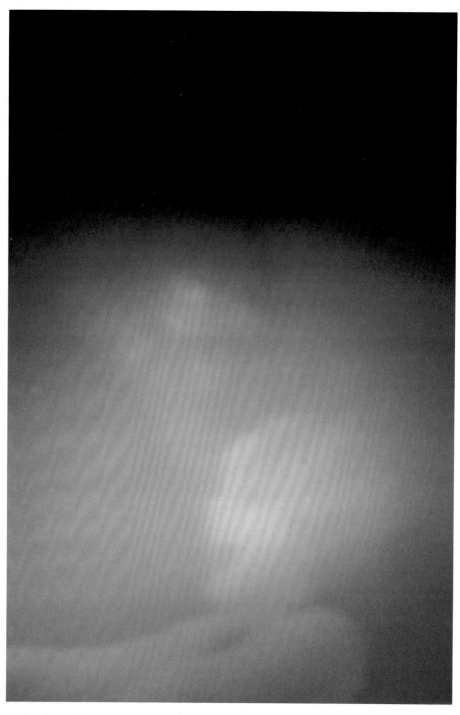

This picture blew me away. Taken on the weekend of my fortieth birthday celebrations, you can see my dad's face just above and to the left of mine. To see him gave me so much comfort and faith. He's with me always. I love you, Dad!

I was pregnant at this point with William from my first marriage, which I went into far too young, and John really looked after me.

Living with John was always amusing. He couldn't stand labels on anything and he used to tear them off. I'd go into the bathroom and be met by all these plain bottles; I didn't have a clue what was in them.

We were having dinner once and John suddenly said to me, 'Don't move!'

'What do you mean?' I asked.

'Do not move. Do not scream.'

As I'm thinking, *What the hell!* to myself, John reached round my shoulder and picked up the most enormous spider with his hands, which had been advancing on me. I always think of all the laughs we had living together whenever I see his name on the credits of something on TV.

I absolutely adored *What's Up Doc?* and we had two very successful years. But then STV decided that they were going to move the show from Maidstone and make it in Glasgow. This caused a huge row with Ged and Vanessa, who absolutely opposed the move.

'Why is it moving to Scotland?' they asked. 'It's giving a lot of work to people in this area and doesn't need to be moved. We're not going.'

STV was equally adamant that the show was moving to Glasgow, so Ged and Vanessa abruptly left. I really couldn't understand it because *What's Up Doc?* was nothing without them. They were the creators and the brains of it.

But that was the end of *What's Up Doc?* in Maidstone and every weekend we were flown up to Glasgow to do the show.

It wasn't the same, though. Everything just fell completely flat. I felt sorry for the new producers because they really tried their best but the spark had been snuffed out.

I desperately tried to help by making suggestions, but for the first time on *What's Up Doc?* I was met with 'No. You're a presenter. You get on with that. We know how to make this show fun.'

Except, they didn't. It wasn't fun at all.

The show had lost its sparkle for me and it was such a long way to travel every week. I started to feel very down about it all.

Just before we had the summer break between series, I met Lulu in Glasgow, who was doing the show with us up there. She was sporting lovely red hair and I complimented her on it.

'My hairdresser in London does it,' she told me. 'Why don't you go to him? I'll speak to him about you and let him know you're coming.'

The salon sent a limo to collect me from my home in Surrey to have my hair done in London, and I couldn't believe it. A limo for a hair appointment? But I loved it.

I was sitting in the salon with a plastic cape round my neck and my hair full of red dye when a salon assistant approached me to say there was a telephone call for me at the desk.

I was puzzled, since hardly anyone knew I was at the salon. I went over to the desk and discovered that the show had somehow tracked me down.

'Yvette,' I was told curtly. 'Don't bother getting the plane to Glasgow for the next show. You're no longer required.'

That was that. It was brutal and there wasn't even any explanation or apology.

I don't know how I managed to get through the rest of that hair appointment. I was in shock. I stepped back into that limo and I cried all the way home.

It was only later that I started to wonder why I'd been given the boot. It was a mystery to me then and, to be honest, to this day I still don't know why I was replaced.

In the event, *What's Up Doc?* only ran for one more series before it was axed. If I'm right, STV had effectively killed it with corporate interference.

Not everyone is so brutal, of course. Ged and Vanessa were wonderful producers, though I've rarely encountered anyone like them on any show I've worked on since. Nor am I suggesting there aren't passionate people like them working in the industry now, but they're the exception and that's a real shame. It's the reason why Karl and I have always tried to play fair with everyone who works for Antix Productions. We know what it's like to be on the other side.

In fact, we've always gone out of our way to help people get a foothold in the industry whenever we can. I'll never forget an incident when I went shopping with Karl for a new vacuum cleaner at the Trafford Centre in Manchester. The young sales assistant recognised us and asked for advice on how to get into television. He was so sincere and eager to learn that we gave him a job at Antix. That's something that I can be proud of when I look back because it was so rewarding.

However, far too many people come into television these days thinking it's a kind of ladder, wondering how far they can get in their career and just ticking off shows that look good on their CVs. What the industry really needs – and is sorely lacking – is those creatives who know what kind of show they want to make and are fired up about it. I love working with people like that because they make the whole job so much more fun to do.

Making television should always be fun because it can often be extremely hard work with terribly unsocial hours. You need a few jokes to keep motivated when you're filming in the pouring rain, knee deep in mud and in the dark at a haunted location. When I look back over all the shows I've done, it's the laughter and the shared absurd moments that stand out most vividly, not the people who disappoint or let you down. That's never more so than on *Most Haunted*. My marriage to Karl is not only based on mutual love and respect but also on a shared sense of humour. He makes me laugh, and I make him laugh.

Laughter can be such a powerful emotion to bring people together – collective laughter is so cathartic. There is, however, an even more powerful one. Perhaps the most powerful of all.

Love.

Shared love can bring the greatest joy a human can experience. The love of a child creates the strongest of bonds. Unrequited love can be excruciating. Thwarted or spurned love can trigger violence or even murder.

We've encountered all versions of the echoes of love in the hauntings we've investigated for *Most Haunted*.

*Chapter 7*

---

# DEAD
# ROMANTICS

*G*RAVEYARDS CAN BE SUCH EVOCATIVE PLACES. I often spend time in Sandbach church, near my home in Cheshire, just looking at all the graves. I'm especially interested in the graves of young children, as so many died at such an early age in the past.

When I look at all those people lying there, I often wonder what stories lie buried beneath the tombstones. Inscriptions can tell us a little. A mother's love for her son, or a devoted couple reunited in death, perhaps. But they can only ever be a hint of what long-forgotten passions and emotions – love affairs, hatred, rivalries and lifelong friendships – those lying in the graves once felt.

Birth and death. Cradle to the grave. These are the two things that every single human being shares. It's what comes between that differentiates us.

There was a wonderful little programme produced in New Zealand once that was shown on the Paranormal Channel, which Karl and I used to own. In it, an investigator would wander around a graveyard, pick out certain graves and then return with a historian to investigate that person's life. Extraordinary stories were unearthed, including that of a man who was the first to go over Niagara Falls in a barrel. He didn't survive to tell the tale.

# Chapter 7

When Karl and I walk past a graveyard, he'll sometimes say, 'This is what it all comes down to. This is the end result. There's no point worrying about this, that or the other because at the end of the day we all end up in the ground or as ashes.'

I have thought about my own funeral and I've told Karl that I want some of my ashes planted under an oak tree, which my daughter Mary will plant. The rest should be put in a bloody big firework so I can go out in a huge blaze of glory.

Not all heightened emotions and passions end when a person dies, however, and they are the trigger behind most of the hauntings we've investigated. It might be a murder victim seeking vengeance; an inherently nasty soul who wishes to torment the living long after they are dead; or the wrongly executed, like George Riley at Shrewsbury Prison, lingering until their innocence can be proved.

However, the strongest human emotion of all is love. While it might be true that the course of true love never did run smooth, as Shakespeare wrote in *A Midsummer Night's Dream*, many of the stories we've investigated have also proved that, in the end, love really is all that matters. These hauntings can be a minefield for serious paranormal researchers, however; people adore a love story, and so these are the types of ghost stories that are most wrapped in myth and legend. Separating those that are false from the truth isn't always easy.

\* \* \*

One of the most affecting love stories we've discovered while making *Most Haunted* was at Bamburgh Castle, Northumberland, in 2006.

Although Northumberland can boast many fine castles, Bamburgh is arguably the most impressive. In fact, as I drove down the road and saw it for the first time, I remember thinking that I hadn't ever seen quite as imposing a place in my life.

Set against a backdrop lined by the stark and stormy waters of the North Sea, the sprawling nine-acre site originally housed a far smaller timber construction than the Norman keep. There's been a castle on the site since at least the sixth century; it was the seat of the kings of Northumbria and was visited by many English kings. Given its location, it was always a strategic castle in the ongoing battles between England and Scotland.

In the eighteenth century, a charitable trust was set up to restore Bamburgh to its former glory; since that time it's been used as a school, a Second World War HQ and a convalescent hospital. With such a long and varied history, it's no surprise that the castle boasts several hauntings from various parts of history.

The unmistakable benign ghost of Dr John Sharp, archdeacon of Northumberland and a renowned philanthropist, who was the first to restore it, has been seen by staff many times wandering throughout the castle that he loved. Witnesses recognise him from his portrait, which hangs in the King's Hall. A very good-looking soldier in the British army uniform of the late 1700s has also been seen regularly. Unseen children are heard running around when there are none on the property, and the sound of a baby has often been heard. An invisible ghost plays a piano, and there are parts of the castle where some people feel terrified, physically sick and even, on occasions, pass out. Dark, eerie shadows lurk in some areas and visitors have often complained of being seized by unseen hands while looking at the portraits.

There's also the Bones Room, which does exactly what it promises on the tin: it's a corner of the castle full of human bones where a tooth was thrown at a member of the *Most Haunted* team after we'd called out for the spirits to do something to let us know they were there.

The tragic tale of the Pink Lady, one of the most famous stories about Bamburgh, tells of a Northumbrian princess whose forbidden love led to heartbreak and her eventually haunting the castle. Her father, the king, sent her lover away for seven years to diminish her feelings, over which time the princess grew despondent. To console her, the king falsely claimed the lover had married someone else and had a pink dress made for her. Overwhelmed, she donned the dress and tragically ended her life by flinging herself from the highest battlements onto the rocks far below. The ghost of the sorrowful girl, clad in her pink frock, supposedly roams the castle every seven years, then stands on the beach, longing for her lost love's return.

It's a colourful yarn of tragic, forbidden love (more myth and fairytale than true history, I suspect) and similar stories, with variations, have been told all over the world. But while stories like these often don't often hold up to close historical scrutiny, there were many credible and reliable accounts of an apparition wearing a pink dress walking at Bamburgh Castle. Whether she had anything to do with the legend, or whether her story was built around sightings of a ghost wearing a pink dress, is probably now lost in time.

It wasn't the Pink Lady's tragic love story that affected me most when we visited Bamburgh, though, but one dating from the Second World War, when the castle was used as a hospital.

\* \* \*

The ghost involved was that of another young soldier, who shot and killed himself while convalescing at Bamburgh. Since his death, he's been seen many times with his head in his hands sitting at the bottom of some stairs in the tapestry passage. People often feel cold spots in the same area, or an icy hand trying to take hold of theirs.

The castle staff told us that the soldier was believed to be called Lionel. He was only identified in the 1980s when two former nurses revisited Bamburgh, where they'd worked during the Second World War, and recognised the details of his terrible suicide at that time. It was thought to have been triggered by a woman.

I was intrigued by why he would choose to tie himself emotionally and physically to the tapestry passage so I decided the team should conduct a séance. What followed was extraordinary and very poignant.

'I don't know what you actually look like,' I called out. 'But I'm trying to imagine what you might have done in your uniform and all the brave things you accomplished during the war. I don't know your circumstances, or if you really killed yourself. Did you kill yourself?'

Some members of the team immediately reported feeling sick as I said this, but I pressed on.

# Chapter 7

'Please help us, Lionel. We won't leave you here, I promise you. We won't leave you without helping you. You will no longer feel the pain, the upset and the sadness. Please talk to us.'

The table started moving.

'Thank you, sweetheart. Why did you kill yourself? Why did you shoot yourself? Is that what you did? Did you shoot yourself in the head?'

The table moved violently, startling the team.

'Don't be frightened,' I told them. 'Get your hands back on the table. That's what we're here to do.' Then I spoke to Lionel again. 'Sorry if we seem startled ...'

The table lurched and juddered even more and that made me hesitate. This was incredible evidence we were getting and it was all being caught on camera. But the activity was becoming much more intense and the energy we could all feel was amazing. None of us really knew where this was going.

'Please keep the contact going, Lionel. Stay with us. You're doing brilliantly. Are you still feeling sad? You were so young. Why did you feel you had to kill yourself?'

There was a noise and the table rocked again.

'Thank you, sweetheart. You're doing so well. That was marvellous. Was it related to a woman?'

We got an affirmative knock.

'Was it someone you loved deeply? Was she killed? Is that correct? The woman you loved was killed in the war?'

The table was now moving and jumping so much that none of us could remain sitting. This was clearly a soul in emotional

164

torment. A heartbroken man. Still feeling the emotional pain in death that he had felt in life.

'Do you want to go to her? Do you want to see her?'

There was a sudden whistle. Often this happens when we've correctly identified something for a spirit – he clearly wanted to follow her.

'What was her name?'

The glass on the table spelled out 'Martha'.

'Do you want to be reunited with Martha?' I asked.

Then the most unexpected thing happened. The table itself started moving towards the stairs. Lionel was leading the table – and us – to the very spot where his ghost has been seen sitting many times.

The movement of the table caught each of us entirely off guard and we were astounded that this spirit was capable of such physical energy. We also felt emotionally drained because we'd discovered the sad explanation behind the reluctance of this tragic soldier to leave the scene of his suicide in the 1940s. His lost love had marked the end of his life. It seemed that, even now, that love was as strong as it was the day he killed himself.

* * *

At another location, we were reminded that love survives death in a way that was to prove much more personal to Karl and me.

Being a mere 800 years old, Fyvie Castle, which stands around 26 miles north of Aberdeen, might be several centuries younger than Bamburgh Castle, but its ghost stories and legends are even more prolific. Now run by the National Trust for Scotland, Fyvie is steeped in Scottish history. But it was Fyvie's dark past that attracted us and some of the castle's darkest stories are very macabre indeed.

The beautifully decorated Morning Room hides a gruesome secret, for it was there that the bones of a young child were discovered when the fireplace was moved in the nineteenth century. Since then, the cries of a young child have been heard in that room and throughout the castle, while the malevolent ghost of a woman, thought to be the child's mother, has been seen wandering the corridors in search of her murdered baby.

The smell of roses inexplicably permeates one bedroom, while another room remains resolutely icy cold, despite all efforts to warm it up. There is also a secret chamber that is said to be cursed. If any laird opens it, a legend predicts, he will die and his wife will go blind. History records that two lairds did, indeed, try to open it but failed. Both died shortly afterwards and both wives suffered eye problems; one did, indeed, go blind. Curse or coincidence? Who can tell? What I do know is that the castle staff weren't taking any chances and refused to give us permission to try to open the chamber ourselves when we were filming there.

The most famous ghost at Fyvie Castle is the Green Lady, who has been seen numerous times over the centuries by many different people. She is believed to be Lilias Drummond, the wife of Alexander Seton, 1st Earl of Dunfermline. When she was accused of adultery, possibly because her husband wanted rid of her to marry someone else, she was locked in a room and starved to death, despite the efforts of her family to rescue her. Some grisly accounts of the story say she saw the dismembered body parts of her slaughtered would-be rescuers dropping past the windows of her locked room.

Although myth and legend have embellished Lilias's tragic story over the years, it's certainly true that she did exist and that she died in May 1601. Her spirit was to make a very personal appearance – at least to Karl and me – during our investigation.

Karl had never been to Fyvie Castle before, and yet from the moment he arrived he felt a strange sense of familiarity, as though he had been there in a previous life.

'As soon as I walked into this place, I felt I could move straight in,' he told me. 'I've not felt scared in any part of this castle and I knew my way around immediately.'

As the investigation got underway, we encountered some familiar happenings after calling out for the spirits to show themselves. A door slammed all by itself. A bed started shaking and moving. And we got the usual raps and noises on the floor. These became much more intense as we contacted the spirit of Lilias Drummond herself.

Communicating through the knocks, Lilias told us that the husband who'd locked her up had done so because he realised that she was in love with another man called Dougal. She was lingering because she wanted to see Dougal again and believed she could see him among our investigation team.

This was a first for us. We'd never experienced anything like it before.

When something kicked Karl on the leg, it seemed that *he* was the object of Lilias's affections. He needed to explore this further, and admitted to me afterwards that he felt very strange asking the questions that he did.

'Do you miss Dougal, or do you miss me? Do I look like Dougal?'

We got affirmative knocks.

'Was your love something that you both wanted to happen but couldn't because you were married?'

Another yes.

We asked Lilias if she would like to marry Karl and if she would be waiting for him when he died.

She again confirmed this.

'She does know you're married to me, doesn't she?' I asked.

Lilias confirmed she did. She made it obvious she didn't like me and wanted Karl nowhere near me because she believed he was supposed to be with her.

'Well, I'm sorry, love,' Karl said firmly, 'but Yvette is my wife and I love her very much.'

Lilias didn't want to hear this and her spirit became very agitated. She was clearly jealous of me, which I found very odd.

This investigation, and many others like it, just underlines how we all want to be loved and accepted. When we're not, it can be the most heart-breaking and devastating emotion. We've encountered many terrible stories of people killing themselves because of unrequited love, sometimes resulting in their unhappy ghosts lingering in the places where they sought happiness.

I feel incredibly lucky to have found happiness with the love of my life, Karl. And I would have fought Lilias across the Ouija board for him if I'd had to!

\* \* \*

Of course, I'd first crossed paths with Karl on *What's Up Doc?*. After STV told me not to return to Glasgow I hit some tough times. I wasn't getting any TV work and I was starting to panic. I was always having to think about paying the mortgage and how to put food on the table, so decided it was time that I pursued teaching.

I'm not quite sure how I managed it now but I secured the position as a drama assistant at a very posh school in Chelsea. It was a beautiful old school and the kids were gorgeous. The headmistress told me I wouldn't be paid for the first two weeks; I would then be assessed and if she decided to keep me, I would receive a salary.

I only lasted a week and a half because, while I was there, I got a call from my agent.

'You've been offered *Dick Whittington* in Tunbridge Wells, Yvette. It's only a short run. Three weeks over Christmas. Do you want to do it?'

I did want to do it but I knew I'd have to clear it with the school first, so I went to see the headmistress to tell her about the offer. As her office was full of photographs of her with various celebrities throughout the decades, I assumed I'd get a sympathetic hearing.

'Listen,' I said. 'I really like this job and I want to carry on doing it. I love helping the kids with the production they're putting on.'

'I can understand that,' she said. 'I've always wanted to be an actress and to be on television, myself.'

*I'm most definitely on safe ground here*, I thought.

'The thing is,' I said. 'I've been offered the part of Dick in *Dick Whittington*. It's only three weeks' work over Christmas and as the school will be closed for the holidays anyway, it won't impact on you at all. Are you happy for me to do it?'

'No.'

I was taken aback by her curt answer.

'Why ever not?' I asked.

'Because you can either be a schoolteacher or a celebrity,' she said, coolly. 'You cannot be both. It's up to you.'

'In that case, I'm terribly sorry,' I said, 'but the panto will pay me more than you're offering so I'm going to have to go.'

I left that day.

Rehearsals for *Dick Whittington* were enormous fun and I took my son William along with me every day. The dancers were always tripping over him. I met some fantastic people on that production and I enjoyed every minute of it. I was also able to put a little money away from that run.

I then started presenting odd little bits here and there for British Forces Television, which I adored because of my love for the military, and then was offered a parenting show with Rowland Rivron for Channel 4 in 1997 out of the blue.

*Baby, Baby* was the perfect show for me to work on at that time. Rowland was a joy to work with, as were the producers. The best thing, though, was that I could take William in with me every day and he would even appear onscreen sometimes. The whole show had a great vibe about it. We filmed it in a three-storey house in London and we had lots of very different parents appearing in each episode.

After that, my career really started to pick up. Topical TV asked me to do a show called *Weekend's Work* for Meridian and that led directly to *City Hospital*, which was the show that changed my life completely.

\*　\*　\*

*City Hospital*, formerly known as *The General*, was a live fly-on-the wall show produced by Topical TV for the BBC, which was broadcast every weekday morning from Southampton General. I presented the first series in 1998 with Chris Searle and Heather Mills.

I must admit we were all scared to death of Heather before she started because we'd been led to believe that she was a real tough businesswoman and something of a tyrant. It was a relief when neither turned out to be true.

I recall one morning when we were both in make-up. We all suddenly became aware of a terrible smell.

'What is that?' one of the make-up ladies asked.

'Smells like burning,' I said.

'Oh my God!' someone exclaimed, tracing the source of the smell. 'It's Heather's leg!'

She'd been standing too close to the heater with her prosthetic leg and it had started to melt.

Working on *City Hospital* was a huge privilege and the number and variety of operations I sat in on was incredible. We had no idea what we would be reporting on from one day to the next, and we got up close and personal with everything that came into that hospital. One minute I'd be watching a Caesarean section, the next I'd be chatting to a man, holding his hand while he was having a benign brain tumour removed.

Prior to seeing my first Caesarean section, the surgeon warned me not to eat anything beforehand and not to look at the first incision because I might faint. I really should have paid more attention to her because, sadly, I *had* eaten when the director started counting down to us going live.

'And we're coming to you in five … four … three …'

The camera was on a close-up of the woman's belly as the surgeon started cutting. I couldn't help watching and then I suddenly started to feel faint and felt myself going. A member of the team caught me and the surgeon looked round to make sure I was okay.

I remember trying to pull myself together, and weakly saying, 'I'm fine,' as professionally as I could.

But then the whole experience took over and just seeing tiny twins coming out of the woman's abdomen was phenomenal.

I'll never forget watching a hip replacement and seeing the staff wheeling in this trolley of equipment that looked like my grandad's toolbox in his garage, right down to the Black & Decker drill. Then I sat there wearing a plastic face shield as bits of cartilage came flying at me.

I got to know the doctors and nurses well and if they saw me even when we weren't filming, they'd say, 'Hi, Yvette. We're just going to do a hysterectomy. Come and watch, if you like.'

I was impressed by how respectful they were of the patients. It reassured me that if I ever had to undergo surgery, I wouldn't be left lying there with my gown thrown over my head for everyone to see.

On one show in 1998, I was presenting an item about how dogs can help people with illness and disabilities; it was this that led to me meeting Karl properly for the first time.

'They've got a patient leaving today and they're being given a dog to help them cope,' the director told Karl, who was the cameraman. 'You'll be doing this item with Yvette.'

What Karl heard was: 'You'll be doing this item with a vet.'

So he was waiting for a professional vet to arrive when I went to him and asked, 'Right, where shall I stand?'

'Don't we have to wait for the vet to come?' he asked.

'No. I'm Yvette.'

And that was our first introduction. He knew who I was because he'd watched me on *Blue Peter* and had worked on *What's Up Doc?*. He just hadn't put two-and-two together that I would be presenting. Karl had worked on everything from *Birds of a Feather* and *Mr Bean* to World Championship boxing since *What's Up Doc?*; he'd been a camera operator on Madonna's 'Frozen' video and had also worked on Michael Jackson and Rolling Stones concerts.

I'll never forget seeing him properly for the first time that day. He was wearing a long-sleeved black T-shirt – which he always wore – and black jeans. He was very lithe and tall and had black hair. He had such charisma, a real presence. I remember looking at him and thinking, *That is the most handsome, sexiest man I have ever seen in my life.*

I'd fallen in love immediately. If I could have had a poster of him on my bedroom wall, I would.

I approached the production team to ask if they could always make sure Karl Beattie was down to be my cameraman when they were planning out who did what on the whiteboard.

'Why?' they asked.

'Because he's the sexiest cameraman in the world,' I said.

'Can't you be just a little bit more subtle?' they suggested.

'Please,' I begged.

They rolled their eyes but said, 'Yes, okay.'

Which is why an unsuspecting Karl 'just happened' to find himself being the cameraman on all my items.

I tried to play it cool at first, but this really backfired on me. When we tried setting up a mutual friend with a soundman and were having a laugh about it all, Karl casually said, 'Maybe I should ask you out or something.'

'Oh, you couldn't handle me,' I said, playing the siren.

In my head, I believed this would make him think, *Flipping heck, of course I can handle her*, and that would be a trigger to him asking me out.

It didn't. Instead, he just shrugged. 'Okay then,' he said and then walked away.

The show finished and I didn't see Karl again until the next series. Still feeling thwarted when production resumed, I started driving the production team mad by wondering what I could do now to get him to ask me out. Even Gaby Roslin, who was also presenting the show at that time, was getting fed up with me. Finally, one of our producers took Karl aside. Thinking he was in trouble, Karl asked what the problem was.

'You need to do something about Yvette.'

'Oh God, I haven't upset her, have I?' Karl asked, mortified.

'No, no. It's not that. She's driving us all nuts. You need to ask her out on a date.'

Finally, he asked, and I had my tarot cards read to make sure he was okay, even though I was sure in my head he was 'the one'.

'I see a very exciting future,' the reader told me. 'You're about to meet somebody special. There's a love interest but you're also going to be tied together working all the time. And I see you both working overseas, including in America. You're going to be working a lot in America.'

Her words rang in my ears later that evening when we were at a restaurant called the Olive Tree in Southampton. At one point, Karl decided to do one of his party tricks, which is to make one eye go one way and one eye go the other way. He was expecting me to react but I didn't. So he was wondering why I wasn't saying anything about him pretending to be boss eyed, while I was sitting there wondering what was wrong with his eyes.

'Have you ever been to America?' I eventually asked him. 'Do you like America … ?'

It turned out he'd not only been to America but had taken himself off there to live for a while when he was younger. He'd even set up his own business teaching martial arts, so he had a lot of experience over there.

\* \* \*

We dated for about three months before Karl famously proposed to me live on-air during an episode of *City Hospital*. I'd been expecting him to do it privately around Christmas time; instead, everyone was in on the act apart from me. The BBC had even alerted the press what he was going to do and we did a photo-shoot afterwards. They also apparently had a mute button ready in case I swore live on air.

I was in an operating theatre – such a romantic setting! – presenting an item with Gaby and suddenly my talk-back mic stopped working. When I asked the sound guy what was wrong, he shrugged, 'Oh, we're having some technical issues.'

I turned to Gaby who just smiled and said, 'We all love you on this show, Yvette. And all your fans love you.'

I was thrown. Why was Gaby suddenly acting so weirdly?

'And we know you've been seeing somebody who works on this show,' she went on. 'One of our cameramen. So here he is now with a lovely bunch of flowers.'

I was still puzzled as I saw Karl approaching with the flowers but assumed he was just going to talk about our relationship.

Then he got down on one knee and proposed. I was like 'Oh my God!' But of course I said yes immediately because I knew I loved him and wanted to spend the rest of my life being married to him.

It was truly magical. The only regret I have about it is that, because it was a total surprise, I was wearing a thick frumpy black sweater that did my figure no favours whatsoever. And that's what I looked like in all the papers the next morning.

I became pregnant with our daughter Mary soon after we were married in 1999 and *City Hospital* wanted me to give birth live on-air. I said no because I preferred it to be a private affair. I didn't want to expose the nation to my privates; I was sure the nation wasn't ready for that. I'm not sure that Mary would have thanked me for it, either.

I was really upset when they didn't ask me back to do another series after that and have always wondered if part of the reason was because I'd said no to showing my vagina on-air. I can't help thinking that Biddy Baxter would have made me do it, otherwise it would have been the Beat Room for me. Come to think of it, I suspect I might have been expected to do the conception live on *Blue Peter*, too!

\* \* \*

After Mary was born, I was asked to present some shows at the Granada Breeze Studios, which was fantastic for me as it wasn't far from that little haunted cottage in Greater Manchester where we lived.

I appeared in all kinds of shows there, including *Girls Talk*, which was a forerunner of *Loose Women*. I felt a bit miffed not to be asked to join the original *Loose Women* panel, as some of the others on *Girls Talk* were, but I let it go as some things are not to be. And if I had done it, maybe I wouldn't have ever made *Most Haunted*, so it worked out for the best.

I loved those years. With the money I was making and what Karl was earning as a high-end cameraman working in the music industry, we were able to build up some savings. We eventually used them to set up our production company Antix Productions and make the pilot for *Most Haunted*.

Antix represents the incredible journey we've been on together for over 20 years, both personally and professionally.

# Chapter 7

Sometimes you see in a movie where a group of people are in jeopardy, whether it's in space, in a war or in a haunted house, and they just must stick together to survive. That's what it's felt like working with Karl.

There's always been the usual minutiae of the running the office and having meetings with executives. But we've always done it as a team. That's how we've always approached it. Sometimes, we haven't known what's going to happen from day to day, so we've always stuck together. I have his back, he has mine. And not once, not for a single day, have we ever treated *Most Haunted* like a television programme. Instead, we've approached every investigation and every single episode as a joint adventure. That's the key to how we work.

If Karl has an idea, I might say, 'Oh my God, I think that's really good.'

Or he might say, 'What do you think?' and I might go, 'I'm not so sure. Can I think about that one?'

Sometimes, of course, an idea might be crap and we tell it as it is.

And on the way home from an investigation, we just talk and talk.

'Can you believe that happened?' Karl will say.

'I know. My God, it was unbelievable.'

There'll be a pause. And then Karl will say, 'Yes, but can you believe that *actually* happened?'

'We caught it on camera,' I'll remind him.

We talk it all through, every investigation, and try to make sense of why it happened. And if an investigation has been particularly scary and left me unnerved, he always looks after me.

'Don't you leave me alone in this house,' I'll say. 'And keep all the lights on.'

He puts on all the lights and says, 'Don't worry, sweetheart. I'll always be here with you.'

And I know he will be because Karl is my soulmate, my best friend, and my hero.

In 2009, ten years after we got married, we renewed our vows in Las Vegas. I wore a 1950s dress and was escorted down the aisle by the best Elvis impersonator, vying with Karl who was also doing his finest Elvis impression because we both adore Elvis Presley. Then ten years after that, we celebrated by getting married again in a church.

We've been so incredibly lucky to create this cultural phenomenon in *Most Haunted*, which so many people all over the world love, within the context of our relationship. I think our secret comes down to mutual respect. I respect everything he does, and vice versa. We support each other 100 per cent. You can meet so many unsavoury characters working in television, and we both have, so it's wonderful to work with someone who loves you and has your back. It was so lucky that we met and fell in love, and I think that comes through in the work we do together.

So the ghost of Lilias Drummond at Fyvie Castle can pine for Karl until eternity for all I care.

I'm going nowhere, because our love is forever. He's my everything.

*Chapter 8*

---

# AMERICAN HORROR STORIES

*W*HEN KARL AND I JOTTED DOWN all our ideas for our proposed new paranormal show, we had no guarantee if we would even get it commissioned. We certainly wouldn't have dared to dream that, in just a few years, we would be broadcasting live episodes of *Most Haunted* for seven hours at a time across the whole of the United States.

But that's what happened.

We didn't plan on making any episodes of the show in the US; it was instead the result of a direct request from the Discovery Travel Channel, who'd broadcast some of the old *Most Haunted* shows as an acquisition from Living. *Most Haunted* had been a great success in the UK. We had, as Arch Dyson predicted, practically saved Living TV from failing and we were always scheduled in the 9pm prime-time slot. We'd been sold to over 100 countries so we knew the series had been seen in America, and we had received some fan mail from there. However, we had no idea just *how* well it had been received.

When the Discovery executives asked if we would make a series of the show in America we soon realised it was because they'd never seen anything like it before.

I must admit that Karl and I did a little jig around the kitchen when they got in touch because this was a whole fresh adventure for us. To be asked to produce an entire series in the USA was unbelievably exciting. Everyone else on the team was ecstatic when they heard the news as well.

Discovery asked if we'd be willing to fly over and meet the team. Too right, we would! So Karl and I travelled to the main Discovery offices in Maryland. We were received in a massive boardroom and there were all these American TV executives who stood up when we entered the room. A very different reception than we got in the UK when we were trying to launch the show. I will confess, that did feel satisfying.

'Oh my God, it's so great to meet you,' they said. 'We've been such huge fans and we can't wait to get things going with you guys over here.'

They showered us with gifts – baseball caps and rucksacks with the channel logo on them – we were honestly made to feel like a visiting king and queen.

They wanted to know how we made the show and seemed gobsmacked when we told them that we just rocked up to a location and filmed an episode within 24 hours.

'What about rehearsals?' they asked.

'We don't do any,' I said.

'What, nothing?'

'No. Everything you see is as it happened, although it's edited down to an hour obviously.'

'You mean you don't fake anything?'

'No. We're not interested in any of that. We stand by everything we show. It's all real.'

They were genuinely astounded and relieved by the fact we didn't fake anything on the show.

*Most Haunted USA* was a big departure for us and it coincided with an evolution in the show itself because by the time we travelled to America to make the new series, our relationship with Derek Acorah had deteriorated badly and would fracture irrevocably shortly afterwards. So now, Derek would just turn up to do his chat on our initial walk round the location and then leave, not taking part in the investigation proper. We used other mediums on these shows.

Part of me would love to return to those locations we visited in the US and investigate them without all the bells and whistles of a medium. When they're on an investigation with you, it's so easy to be overly influenced by what they say. For instance, if the medium says, 'I've got a John here,' suddenly the whole investigation becomes centred around trying to speak to a John. I find it's better to use your own senses and equipment, and that the most convincing and positive evidence for us as an investigation team is the knocking phenomenon where the spirits can give you their own messages. I know that's coming from the other side. So I think we'd get even better results now if we went back to some of our old filming locations; even places in the UK, such as the Theatre Royal, Drury Lane, say, would be so much more fascinating with a smaller investigation team and all the experience we now have behind us.

I must admit I did feel very emotional at times when we were filming in America. Sometimes, when I was alone with

Karl in the hotels, I'd even cry occasionally. But these were tears of pride, not sadness. It was hard to think that this show, which Karl and I had devised, writing down ideas on sheets of paper scattered across the bed, had brought us all the way to America. I can even get emotional thinking about that now because I felt such joy about what we'd achieved together and how well it was doing.

Even before we arrived there to film, American audiences had really taken us to their hearts and were heavily invested in the show. It proved to me just how much people right across the world yearn to know if there is life after death. We'd get so many people in the US coming up to us to thank us, saying things like they now knew their mother, brother, daughter or whatever was happy and safe on the other side. That did it for me. It was wonderful to know we were giving people hope.

So much for that broadcaster telling us we were unprofessional for even thinking about making a paranormal show.

Discovery had also taken a live feed from one of our UK live shows and it done so well with their audience that they asked if we'd do some US live shows in addition to the regular episodes we were making for them. They wanted to make one big change, however.

'So Yvette and Karl, you know how you do your live shows as three-hour broadcasts back home,' they said. 'How would you feel about doing seven hours live straight over here?'

'Seven hours live across the USA, are you kidding me?' I asked.

'Sure. We'd love you to do it.'

I was a little wary about saying yes at first because I'd never broadcast live for such a length of time before or to such a potentially huge audience. If it went wrong, there would be a lot of egg on my face. I was still troubled by memories of having to get through three hours presenting a *Most Haunted Live* from a very un-haunted Midland Grand Hotel in London. It's now the very plush and beautiful Renaissance Hotel St Pancras, but back then it was empty and parts of it were derelict. It was only being used occasionally, mostly as a film location: the music video of the Spice Girls' 'Wannabe' was shot there.

The site was chosen by the production company that Living TV had imposed on us to produce some of our earliest live shows, and Karl and I knew from the outset that it was a mistake. We argued there were no ghost stories or a tradition of any hauntings there, but we were overruled. I've no idea why, maybe they were keen to film there because it looked so grand onscreen and was in the centre of London. But that's no reason to base a live ghost hunt in a place where there is absolutely no record of it being haunted at all.

I struggled terribly that night, presenting three long hours of absolutely nothing happening being broadcast live. It was awful. I've never padded a show as much as I did then, wandering around with Derek. I can't now remember what he was coming out with, although I recall I wasn't very convinced by any of it. I kept thinking to myself, *I'm so bored by this place.* And if I was bored, I knew the audience would be, too. I was worried no one would ever watch *Most Haunted* again after it, and was lucky I was wrong.

## Chapter 8

What if the same thing happened in America and I had *seven* hours to fill? I was cautious, but Karl and I knew this was a huge moment for *Most Haunted* and so, of course, we agreed.

\* \* \*

The first American live show we did was from the Eastern State Penitentiary in Philadelphia in 2007. If I wasn't nervous before I arrived, the drive to the location didn't help to calm me. It was one of the scariest places any of us had ever been in our lives; 75,000 men and women had been condemned to spend the rest of their lives within its bleak walls, which was enough to make us apprehensive.

Opened in 1829 to try to change the behaviour of criminals through solitary confinement and hard labour, the intention was one of reforming vision but the reality was that it became a place of despair, mental illness, death and even torture. The imposing gothic outer walls housing the main entrance and admin block would have been a prisoner's first sight of the penitentiary, and were deliberately designed to strike terror into the heart of any offender. Brick entry boxes, complete with machine guns, were installed in the 1920s, finally dispelling any vestiges of the earlier ideals of penitence and rehabilitation. By then only the most hardened and dangerous criminals were housed here. Strict discipline was enforced, and would often involve the withholding of basic human rights. It was finally closed as a prison in 1971.

The police had cordoned off all the roads leading up to its entrance for our filming and there were huge cheering crowds greeting us. They were so enthusiastic that Paul Ross, who was hosting the show as he had done on some of the lives back home, saw one American fan eagerly scoop up a cigarette butt tossed aside by one of the electricians to save as a souvenir.

'I don't think you'll get much for that on eBay, mate,' Paul quipped.

The scale of that production was unlike anything we'd ever had before. I was even given my own Winnebago. The Americans had their own team already installed and there must have been about 50 of them, a number that dwarfed the team we usually used on the UK shows.

We did a walk around the prison with the US team to get acquainted with the area and, as usual, the knockings and tapping started up even before we'd asked for any activity.

'What's that?' the Americans asked.

'That's just paranormal activity,' I explained. 'They're letting us know where the haunted areas are.'

Their soundman was having none of it. 'I know how you guys are doing this,' he kept repeating as he tore up floorboards, clearly determined to prove we were faking it.

There was a cupboard in one of the rooms where some of the most frantic knocking was coming from. The soundman yanked open the door and was stunned to find there was no one inside. He just couldn't accept that it was real.

I'd felt full of trepidation ever since we had agreed to doing these live shows and by the day of that first one, I was physically shaking with nerves and smoking a lot. I used to smoke back then – actually, I must confess I still do, although only at weekends – and I think I got through a whole packet ahead of going live.

# Chapter 8

The facilities were quite rudimentary. Remember, this was an abandoned prison where men on Death Row awaited execution, sometimes for years. It was desolate and unpleasant, and being on air for seven hours meant I had to take a break for a wee whenever I could. The only place I could go was some kind of exercise yard, which was now covered in weeds. The poor make-up lady had to hold a torch for me during the commercial break and I'd whip down my trousers and flip up the back of my long black coat to have a quick wee while I heard the ads playing in my earpiece. It was quite a humiliating experience, and I'm glad I didn't find out until much later that the yard was where the prison authorities unceremoniously buried all the unclaimed bodies of the men they'd executed.

I have to say, though, that the Eastern State Penitentiary was one of the best live shows we've ever done in any country.

At the time we visited, it was a truly horrific and decaying location. It was also humid and stormy when we were there, with lightning and thunder punctuating the night sky, and parts of the building had the most awful and grim atmosphere.

Some of us felt like we'd been grabbed and we seemed to contact the horrifying ghost of a man who'd had his throat cut. I can still remember vividly going into Al Capone's old cell, where we put a barrel of water on top of a table and trained a camera on the water. You could see it rippling as the table moved of its own accord.

The viewing figures for the show were phenomenal and the channel told us they were the best numbers they'd ever known. In fact, Discovery were so blown away by how well that show did that they wanted us to do more live shows.

I'll never forget how the whole America crew gave us a standing ovation when we came off air. As for the fans, oh my God, they treated us like The Beatles. It was the same wherever we went. When we did a live show from Gettysburg in 2008, where so many soldiers had died in battle in the American Civil War, people booked out all the hotels and B&Bs just so they could watch us making it. They would scream and shout for us, carry placards and hang banners out of the windows saying, 'We Love Most Haunted'.

When we did a live show from the Winchester House in San Jose, California, we were intrigued by the sound of loads of people coming from outside.

'I think you need to go out there,' the head of production told us.

'Why?' I asked.

'You have to see what's going on,' she said.

We had a peek and saw a huge crowd of people outside. Hundreds of them. 'Is there some kind of parade going on?' I asked.

'No,' she grinned. 'That's all for you.'

'Sorry?' I said, 'I don't understand.'

'They're your fans. And they've come to see you.'

I was stunned. It blew my mind. All those people, with their banners and placards, and their hands stretching through the bars to grab a photograph with Karl and me or to get an autograph, was something I'd never experienced. It was on a completely different level from anything we'd known in the UK. Here the fans are more reserved but in America the energy of the people who turned out for us was unreal.

Even now, I don't quite understand why people want my autograph or to be photographed with them. I'm just me, and don't think of myself as a celebrity. But I do love chatting to everyone and hearing about pictures of ghostly shapes or orbs they've caught on camera. I'm happy talking to people for hours about their experiences. I've sometimes even been told off by production teams when I've stayed talking to fans for too long and it's held up filming.

A measure of just how popular *Most Haunted* had become in the US was when we were parodied on *Saturday Night Live* in October 2006. *SNL*, as it's known, has been running since 1975 and is a mix of stand-up, political satire and sketch-show comedy. It's a cultural phenomenon that has seen its sketches turned into huge movies like *The Blues Brothers* and *Wayne's World*, and has starred performers like John Belushi and Dan Ackroyd, Bill Murray and Eddie Murphy, Mike Myers, Adam Sandler and Jason Sudeikis.

Like the rest of the team, I was both gobsmacked and excited when I heard about the sketch and saw who would be involved.

'Hugh Laurie is playing Derek Acorah on *Saturday Night Live*,' Karl said. '*Hugh Laurie!* Can you believe that?'

It was a huge deal for us and proof, if we needed any more, that we'd really arrived in America.

I'm not sure if Derek ever saw that sketch, or what he thought of it if he did. I do know that he absolutely hated the send up French and Saunders had done of us a couple of years before *SNL* did theirs.

Their skit was based on an investigation we did in the early days of *Most Haunted* when the team had gone into the ladies' toilets at one location. The hand dryer went off and I screamed my head off and that was it. Dawn French played Derek and Jennifer Saunders played me. They got us down to an absolute T but they insinuated that Derek was getting his information through an earpiece, which was possibly closer to the truth than any of us knew at the time.

We were doing a live show at the time the sketch went out but the head of Living TV had recorded it and played it to us at breakfast in the hotel the next morning. We all sat watching it and I saw that while Karl, the crew and I were rolling around with laughter, Derek's face was fit to burst. He was not happy. Not happy at all.

Personally, I thought that the French and Saunders parody was hilarious and a huge compliment. I really don't mind people making fun of me or the show. I've survived Biddy Baxter and everything the paranormal can throw at me, so I've got a thick skin!

Billy Connolly used to do a bit about us in his stand-up act. 'Have you seen *Most Haunted*?' He'd say. 'With that English woman with the blonde hair and that Liverpool fake that's with her? Him that has the guru that you can't see. He's talking to this fucking non-person!'

I never minded that because I absolutely adore Billy Connolly. Along with Morecambe and Wise he's one of my all-time comic heroes. I even have a photograph of him on my wall at home. I had the chance to meet him when Karl bought tickets for one of his shows for my birthday once. I saw him signing autographs outside the theatre and I wanted to go and speak but I held back because I didn't want this comic hero of mine saying I was a crackpot or I was nuts. Not that I think he would, he's too much of a gentleman and a professional for that.

In any event, Karl had had a quiet word with Billy's agent ahead of the performance and said, 'Just to let you know, Yvette will be in the audience tonight.' Billy took out the 'bloody blonde woman' bit. Mind you, some members of the audience recognised me when we left the theatre afterwards and gave me a bit of good-natured banter about what Billy said about *Most Haunted* in his show. I didn't care because just the thought that Billy Connolly knew about my show, whether he loved or hated it, made my day.

\* \* \*

Whenever I think about *Most Haunted USA*, my thoughts always return to the two-parter we filmed aboard the *Queen Mary* in Long Beach, California. It's arguably the most memorable location we've investigated anywhere.

The *Queen Mary* is one of the most famous ships in the world. Built for Cunard in Clydebank, Scotland, in the 1930s, she was the pride of the ocean, epitomised the Art Deco style and was a true British icon. The *Queen Mary* served both as a luxury liner for royalty and A-list guests and as a troop carrier in the Second World War, ferrying Allied troops and German prisoners-of-war. Indeed, during the war she was known as 'the Grey Ghost' and because of her speed of nearly 30 knots, she could outpace the German U-boats, meaning she was perfect to whisk Winston Churchill across the Atlantic to the US and Canada for meetings several times. Churchill loved the *Queen Mary* so much that he dubbed her his 'headquarters at sea'. No wonder Adolf Hitler promised the Iron Cross and a small fortune to any of his bomb crews who could sink her. They never succeeded.

The *Queen Mary* resumed duties as a passenger ship after the war but when the transatlantic business waned, she was sold and sailed to her final resting place in Long Beach, California, where she opened as a hotel, restaurant and museum in the early seventies.

The *Titanic* was known as 'the ship of dreams', but the *Queen Mary* is surely the ship of hauntings: not only is she reputed to hold more ghosts than any other ship in the world, but she's also said to be the sixth most-haunted property in the whole of the United States. There are 55 documented deaths associated with the *Queen Mary* – 38 of them passengers – but that figure might be much higher given that some of the prisoners-of-war were held in terrible conditions and no one really knows how many soldiers, sailors and airmen might have perished in the dark bowels of the ship.

Given her haunted reputation, the *Queen Mary* was an obvious place for us to investigate while we were filming in the States and, at more than a thousand feet long, also a mammoth one. We were so lucky to be given the opportunity to have the ship to ourselves for three weeks in total. This was unprecedented, not only for us but for all paranormal broadcasting because no other ghost show on television had ever been given such free access to a location before. Not only did we get the chance to do a thorough investigation there but also to live aboard. We spent one week onboard, then we travelled off to other US locations and stayed in several hotels, before coming back to the *Queen Mary* for about two more weeks.

For a relatively modern haunted location you're knee-deep in ghosts on the *Queen Mary*. The figure of a man in 1930s clothes has been seen many times by guides and guests alike in the first-class lounge. Lights turn themselves on and off in the bedroom areas. People have heard heavy breathing in the dead of night and even felt the bedclothes pulled off them. The ghost of a woman in a long, flowing gown has been seen dancing to an unseen, silent orchestra. Best of all is B Deck, which is every ghost hunter's dream with its reported activity, especially Room B340, which was never let out to paying guests back then, despite the loss of revenue, because of its horrific ghosts.

Karl and I took William and Mary with us on that trip to Long Beach, which was something of a departure for us; they'd usually stay at home with the nanny or my mum when we were on the road. They were terribly excited and it was such a treat for Karl and me to have them with us. They were still too young to really understand what we did for a living and we tried to keep them away from the paranormal as much as we could. They knew about some of it, of course, but I always said to them, 'Oh, we make it up. It's like a drama.'

The reason I did that was because I didn't want them worrying or being scared if someone at school said to them, 'I saw your daddy collapse on television last night.'

We had a double room when we stayed on the ship, with an open door to a bathroom, and the kids' room was on the other side. Every night we were there, without fail, I would hear the overhead light click on in William and Mary's room, followed by footsteps going around their beds, through the bathroom and then into our room.

Mary was about six or seven then and my instinct when I first heard the footsteps was that she'd got up and needed something. So I got out of bed to see if everything was okay. When I got in the room, though, I found that she and William were sleeping soundly, although the light was on and was shining very brightly. That happened every single night. And every night I had to go and turn that light off.

Most of the members of our crew slept on the *Queen Mary* for that investigation as well and I think every one of them experienced some paranormal activity of one kind or another.

However, there was one place we all knew we had to investigate: Room B340 – the infamous room which was blocked off because people were too scared to sleep there. That was a challenge we couldn't resist, so we asked our crew, 'Right, who's brave enough to sleep in this room?'

No one wanted to volunteer.

'Okay, we'll buy you an alcoholic beverage of your choice if you do it.'

Still no takers.

'A bottle, then.'

Eventually one brave soul put his hand up. He later admitted he had to get tipsy before he went in the room because he was so frightened.

We'd rigged up the room with cameras and, to this day, the footage of what happened in that cabin that night freaks me out.

You can see him being woken up by footsteps. Then you hear the clanging of metal coat hangers moving on their own. And then you hear the voice of a little girl clearly saying: 'Mummy.'

That was particularly chilling because Room B340 was right at the end of the corridor and we knew there were no children aboard apart from William and Mary, who were accounted for.

It wasn't just the ghosts that woke us up at ungodly hours, though. During one of the weekends when we came back to the *Queen Mary* after filming in other locations around the US, we were rudely disturbed by the sound of strangled bagpipes.

Not just one, but hundreds of them.

Unbeknownst to us, the *Queen Mary* was hosting a celebration of all things Scottish where US citizens who felt they had even the most tenuous link to Scotland came to connect with their inner William Wallace and Bonnie Prince Charlie for the whole weekend. We were plagued with the sight of hairy American men dressed in kilts squeezing bags under their arms and making the most frightful sounds.

They liked to walk up and down the dock outside the ship at dawn, wailing and shouting and playing the bagpipes. We weren't entirely sure which was the scarier: American men playing the bagpipes or the ghosts in B340.

We were also kept awake some nights by our frisky crew members. I don't know if it was the sea air or working in laid-back California but that investigation proved to be something of an aphrodisiac for them. In fact, at times the *Queen Mary* was more like the *Love Boat* while we were there. Our team weren't immune to the love bug either. One member of the crew even flew their spouse over to join us!

'My God, what's going on with everybody?' I asked Karl at one point. 'It's like this ship has cast some kind of magic spell.'

Karl and I were seemingly unaffected. We were the only ones who had children with us, so we were like the two boring old farts all through that investigation.

As for the others, let's just say it was a case of what happened onboard the *Queen Mary* stayed onboard the *Queen Mary*!

The paranormal activity didn't abate. The *Queen Mary* just kept delivering and towards the end of our investigation was about to provide us with some of the most compelling evidence we had filmed up to that point.

On one vigil, we all heard distinct footsteps and saw unexplained lights; some of us felt we were being grabbed or touched; and we had constant interference with the walkie-talkies, which is how we kept in contact with the different members of the investigation team. This was something that none of us had ever experienced before and was extremely disturbing.

We then investigated the deepest bowels of the *Queen Mary*, including the dark void eight fathoms below the waterline where the huge engines had once stood as well as the first-class swimming pool, which had long since been drained of any water.

Using a thermal-imaging camera in what had been the purser's office, I saw a patch of red, which indicated heat, on the top of a chair that no one had been near. It looked like a handprint, as though someone unseen had placed their hand there.

A little later, a bathroom or swimming-pool tile was hurled at members of the team, leaving them stunned. Only five members of the team were in that part of the ship and each one was a least

30 yards from the incident, meaning none of them could have thrown it.

However, the *Queen Mary* had saved her best until we investigated the former first-class swimming pool. From the moment we got there, I kept seeing in the corner of my eye something or someone running around the top of the pool area, but every time I looked properly, I just kept missing whatever it was. I also heard something breathing very close to me, which was very unnatural.

And then Jon Gilbert, our soundman, suddenly spoke up.

'I've just seen someone,' he said.

'What?' I asked.

'I tell you I saw someone,' he repeated. 'Sitting on the edge of the slide over there.'

'You're kidding!' I said, 'Are you sure?'

'Yes.'

'Are you all right?'

'Yeah,' he said. It was clear he was. Anyone watching that footage can see he wasn't in the least bit scared. Instead, he had a half smile, as though he was pleased to have finally seen a full apparition.

'What did it look like?' I asked.

'A woman wearing white swimwear. This is incredible. I've never experienced anything like this before.'

We were all keen to see for ourselves the woman Jon had seen. We didn't. But what we *did* see was just as incredible because it became clear that she had left behind a trail of water up the stairs leading from the pool. There was great excitement among the team as we kept finding patches of water, seven in total, and most clearly in the shape of footprints.

When we looked more carefully, we saw the prints had been made by small, bare feet that most likely belonged to a woman. The thing was, though, there was no water in the pool and there hadn't been for years. Also, every single member of the team could be accounted for and none of them could have made those prints without being seen.

So who had made them and how?

When the water dried, it left behind a salt residue. Only later did we establish that the pool used to draw its water from the ocean.

It was one of the most compelling pieces of footage we'd ever obtained and even though it wasn't a controlled experiment as such, even our sceptical parapsychologist couldn't explain it and was prepared to admit, at long last, that it could be considered genuine paranormal activity.

The *Queen Mary* is one of my favourite locations we've ever visited. I love that ship and all her history. Even without the paranormal activity we captured, I will never forget those three weeks. Sometimes I'd just take a walk on the decks with a coffee and wonder who'd walked on those planks of wood before me. All those film stars and members of royalty. Walking where Winston Churchill had walked while he was steering our nation to victory. It really did feel like stepping back in time when you went aboard because the rooms were exactly as they had been back in the 1930s and 1940s, and when you went to breakfast or lunch, they'd pipe out big band music.

\*    \*    \*

I'd love to go back and investigate the *Queen Mary* again, but there are also so many other locations I'd like to visit as well, not just in America but also Europe. People often assume that the UK has a monopoly on hauntings because of our rich history, but that's not the case. We've proved that by investigating the USA, Italy, the Czech Republic and even Transylvania. I'd love to investigate New Orleans, for instance. What a tragic history that city has, and now houses are being built on burial grounds. It also has a rich history of voodoo. I believe voodoo is real and it's something I want to see and investigate myself.

Then there's the Myrtles Plantation in Louisiana, which has a horrible history of slavery and abuse and is said to be badly haunted. Just imagine the number of souls there who need help.

The frustration is that to film abroad, to pay the crew decently and to make a show professionally costs a great deal of money. On top of that, some of the most suitable places now demand ridiculous sums just for a camera crew to spend the night there and use them as a location. To do it properly, you need the backing of a channel.

And sadly, the television industry in the UK is in a terrible state, both financially and creatively. Probably the worst it's ever been. Look at what the BBC did to *Blue Peter*. They took it off BBC One and replaced it with *Pointless*, which is a good show if you like game shows. But then they moved *Blue Peter* to CBBC where no one watches it.

Why did they do that? *Blue Peter* isn't just a TV show, it's a flagship institution that people have watched for over 60 years. Kids would come home from school and sit down with their families while it was on. That's all gone now and it really annoys me. Obviously, I'm passionate about *Blue Peter* and it's hard for me to be totally objective, but I think it's such a shame. And it's not just *Blue Peter*.

There used to be so many good shows on every channel but they've all gone now. Where are the great days of Morecambe and Wise when the nation was wetting itself collectively on a Saturday night or on Christmas Day? When was the last brilliant sitcom like *Only Fools and Horses* or *Rising Damp*?

It's not that the talent isn't there but most performers and writers of comedy are terrified of saying anything in case they're cancelled. Obviously, there must be a balance, but there always was. There is no balance now. What's happened is that a vocal minority has ruined television for the majority.

As for the commissioning process, it is now mainly old university mates scratching each other's backs. It's no wonder to me that a lot of people have abandoned mainstream television altogether and watch Netflix or Amazon.

What makes it all worse is that the accountants have taken over from the creatives, and all broadcasters are interested in now is in penny-pinching, spending as little money on shows as they can get away with. That's why most of the paranormal shows are now being produced in the USA or by the huge streaming services like Apple TV+ or Paramount+. Those American shows have huge budgets whereas British networks have all but thrown in the towel. Isn't it a shame that *Most Haunted*, the show that started it all, has been pushed aside by the American shows?

Sadly, I can't see that changing any time soon. However, nothing can take away what we achieved with those American episodes. *Most Haunted USA* remains a unique part of the show's history and of our paranormal journey. I'll never forget the locations we visited, the spirits we encountered and, most of all, the American fans who took us to their hearts and made those shows so successful.

I also recall that tarot card reader who, ahead of my first date with Karl, predicted I was about to meet someone I'd work with constantly and that, together, we would work in America and find success there.

How right she was. But what she didn't predict was that we would talk to the dead.

## Chapter 9

# TALKING TO THE DEAD

*I*S IT POSSIBLE TO TALK TO THE DEAD?

Thomas Edison, one of the most famous and prolific inventors in history, certainly thought so and, in October 1920, he told a prestigious American magazine that he was working on a spirit phone.

'I have been at work for some time building an apparatus to see if it is possible for personalities which have left this earth to communicate with us,' he told them. 'If this is ever accomplished, it will be accomplished not by any occult, mystifying, mysterious or weird means, such as are employed by mediums, but by scientific methods. It will cause a tremendous sensation if successful.'

Edison certainly believed that life was indestructible, and theorised that our personalities have a physical form comprising tiny entities like atoms that might survive after death and retain the essence of who a person was in life.

There's some mystery as to what happened to the prototype machine Edison was working on but I find it telling that this renowned, respected and highly intelligent scientist not only believed in life after death but was convinced that we could communicate with the dead, perhaps using a different frequency.

Thomas Edison died before his theories were properly developed but I'm sure he'd be intrigued to see how the electronic voice phenomenon has evolved into such a crucial and fascinating branch of paranormal investigation. Since his death, many researchers have explored white noise, which sounds like a hissing sound you get when a radio or TV doesn't have a clear signal. For some bizarre reason, the spirits seem to be able to use white noise to communicate with us; we can hear their voices or even speak to them.

EVP recording has been adapted and refined over the years so that now you can get apps for your laptop or smartphone to use in a haunted location or even your own home to speak to a deceased loved one. You won't hear any noises with your own ears, but you'll see on the sound waves that something has made a blip and caused the soundwaves to peak. Once you amplify that sound, you might hear something along the lines of, 'Hello, it's grandma …' You can even leave your phone recording by the side of your bed overnight, although I've been too scared to do it, and check the next morning to see if there are any blips in the waveform; you could be talking in your sleep or snoring, but it could also be a voice from the other side.

We've had some extraordinary results from using EVP recording during the years of doing *Most Haunted*, and it's one of my favourite ways of communicating with the other side. One of the most interesting occurred at the Birmingham Steelhouse Lane Lock-Up, a Grade II-listed former police station and grim prison which opened in 1891 and didn't close until 2016.

A year after that closure, we were filming in another part of the building but left a camera and an EVP computer recording in a cell. I called out all the past women prisoners' names that we knew about, just to see if we'd get a reaction. We got the usual bumps and knocks, but when we returned to the EVP computer there was much more. When we played back what the EVP had recorded, we could hear a woman crying. It was tragic. And then we heard, 'No. No. No.'

That was awful because I could hear the trauma in her voice. Her obvious sadness made me emotional and I wanted to cry because of her distress.

At the Leopard Inn in Burslem in Staffordshire, we called out to the room and seemingly got no reply, but the EVP clearly picked up a child's voice saying 'Hello.'

On another occasion, this time at the Tivoli Venue in Buckley, North Wales, we were conducting a Ouija board session and the exact same words it was spelling out were also being spoken simultaneously by a man's voice on the EVP machine. I asked if there was a spirit with us. The board spelled out 'Yes' and we heard a voice say 'Yes'. I asked if the spirits belonged to that place. Again, the board and a voice confirmed simultaneously. I asked for the spirit's name. We heard 'Harry' on the EVP machine as the board spelled out the same name. That was just incredible. And at Shrewsbury Prison, where 63 people were hanged between 1795 and 1961, the EVP picked up the very distinct words 'execution' and 'rescue me'.

On one of our investigations of the Witch's House at Pendle Hill, we were all downstairs while the EVP was upstairs. I was calling out for the spirits to do something, and that generated some thuds and knocks. But when we checked the EVP, we heard the distinct sound of a child or a young woman, maybe, whimpering a couple of times plus the sound of someone breathing. Everyone on the investigation team was on camera and accounted for: none of us was even close to the EVP recorder as we were on a different floor.

Sometimes, the voices the EVP recordings pick up can be threatening, even terrifying. We were conducting a séance at the 300-year-old Church Farmhouse in Skegness and had the EVP recorder running. One of our investigators asked, 'Where are you sitting?'

'Behind you,' said a voice on the EVP.

That was freaky.

The most chilling result we had from EVP (with the exception of Elizabeth Demdike in the Aldwych Underground station) happened at 30 East Drive in Pontefract, which is one of the most active haunted locations we've ever visited. At one point, I was in the bedroom with a couple of other members of the team, and Karl and Stuart were downstairs in the lounge. The door was open and I was calling out to Carl Anthony, a former priest and a very negative energy who haunts the property.

He spelled out his name via knocking on the board and gave us the dates he was there. Then you clearly hear his voice on the film and on the EVP recording.

'Shut the door,' he said, very calmly.

Although we were alarmed by this, we did shut the door and then all hell broke out in the rest of the house. He had clearly wanted to separate us by getting us to close the door and that felt very threatening.

Our EVP evidence has been remarkably convincing over the years. We've recorded lots of different words and even complete sentences. Sometimes they're female voices. Other times male, or even children. And for me, to know that no one is in a locked room with the EVP recorder and then to hear someone breathing, speaking or even giving their name is simply astonishing. You can't dispute that. To my mind, it's proof positive that the paranormal is real and that we can communicate with the dead.

EVP and recordings of the dead have been going on for very many years now and the technology is improving all the time. If we keep going at this rate, I wonder if we'll all be picking up our iPhones in a few years and speaking to our departed loved ones.

\* \* \*

While we've had great success at communicating with spirits through EVP and Ouija boards on *Most Haunted*, the jury is still out on whether the mediums we've used have talked to the dead or not. I can only speak from my experience as it's not for me or anyone else to judge on the veracity of mediumship any more than it is to question if a vicar or priest is truly speaking to God. That said, anyone can draw their own conclusions from the decision Karl and I made to dispense with mediums completely in our later series of *Most Haunted* in favour of more serious research, having been severely let down by one in particular.

The first warning signs that things weren't all as they seemed with Derek Acorah came early. We were happy that he'd chosen to join us for the pilot in 2001; but just before we started filming it one of the presenters at Granada Breeze who'd worked with him previously came up to me in the make-up room and asked if she could have a word. She asked the make-up lady to leave and closed the door so she could speak privately.

'You simply can't use Derek Acorah on your show,' she said.

Thrown by this, I asked why not.

'I'm warning you, he's a fake,' she stated firmly. 'I know he's a fake and I know how he gets all this supposed spiritual information he comes up with on his show.'

I must admit, I became a bit defensive. Perhaps naively.

'I'm really sorry,' I said, 'but that's only your opinion. I'm impressed by what I've seen of him so we're going to use him.'

And it was true. I really was genuinely convinced by Derek. At that time.

'Well, on your own heads be it,' she said. 'I just wanted to let you know what I think. So I can only wish you all the luck in the world using him.'

How we were to wish many times in the next five or so years that we'd listened to her advice.

Living TV loved that pilot, as we know, and commissioned the first batch of 16 episodes. Well, they loved everything about it that is, with one great big caveat:

Derek.

'You need to change the medium,' they told us. 'He's too end-of-the-pier. Dump him.'

We had no intention of dumping Derek because we liked him back then. However, we really did have to fight the channel hard to keep him in that first series.

We were also aware that their 'end-of-the-pier' criticism wasn't entirely without merit because, as I've said, Derek did exhibit a certain flamboyance in those days. We encouraged him to pull back on his image a bit by having his mullet cut and wearing smarter jackets in less vibrant colours.

Derek was happy to listen to us because he was just so grateful that we'd given him the opportunity to work on *Most Haunted* and I must admit we had very few problems with him during the first series.

It was during the making of that first series of *Most Haunted* that we first experienced Derek's supposed possessions, in which he would claim to be taken over temporarily by whichever spirit he'd supposedly contacted. In fact, the very first of these happened in the filming of our pilot show at Michelham Priory. They were very popular with the audience and the executives wanted him to deliver more and more of them each series. I'm convinced this is what fuelled many of the problems we had with him later down the line.

It's worth reiterating that at that time Karl and I firmly believed Derek really was genuine. The whole crew did. All I knew about possessions was what my mum had told me about going to see *The Exorcist*, which was all about demonic possession. She'd described the priests and the nuns protesting outside the cinema and imploring people not to go in, and the ambulances waiting to treat cinemagoers who'd fainted with shock.

So when I saw Derek standing in a doorway at Michelham Priory with his face contorting and his voice becoming a menacing growl, I was shaking with fear. This was the real-life *Exorcist* as far as I was concerned. I'd never seen anything like it before and I believed it. We all did because it was fantastically good and convincing to witness. It was also frightening because it wasn't like sitting in a theatre watching a medium onstage from the stalls; I was standing right next to Derek.

He was allegedly possessed again when we filmed at the Theatre Royal, Drury Lane, and if you watch either of those episodes again you can see just how alarmed I look. I wasn't scared for Derek as such, but for myself and the crew. When you're standing so close to a big, strong man like Derek who has apparently been taken over by an entity and is spitting and growling and spewing out weird, harsh words, you don't know what's going to happen next.

Derek always told us not to be afraid when he became possessed because he claimed he had a spirit guide with him always.

'Never be scared when I go into these things,' he'd say. 'I've been doing this for years now. And Sam's there to protect me. So you must never worry that anything bad is going to happen to you.'

Derek's reassurances helped a little because I believed in him. Even so, I hated being close to him when he became possessed. I hated his 'possessions' more in later series, but for very different reasons.

When Derek wasn't being possessed, he could be extremely good company that first year. We were travelling long distances on the road between locations and he'd always mix socially. None of us knew if the show would even last beyond one series and he had as much riding on it as Karl and I did, so we were a real team.

We had no inkling at the time that Derek was a man battling his own personal demons. These were demons that had nothing to do with the paranormal and in the next five years the whole *Most Haunted* team, but Karl and myself most acutely, would be caught in the crossfire.

In retrospect, I suppose the signs were there from the beginning. I recall once, early in our association with Derek, that we were having a small private dinner in Holland. He was a bit drunk and he stood up, put his arms out like he'd been crucified on the cross and proclaimed that he was Jesus, that he was the Second Coming. He then proceeded to chase me round the restaurant, and I was batting him away because he was trying to ram his tongue down my throat. Derek was always trying to snog me.

We just laughed off that night. We all rolled our eyes and thought Derek's had a bit too much to drink. We were to discover subsequently that Derek and alcohol were not a good mix. Drink always changed him. It loosened him up and then the 'possessions' would become more extreme. I don't believe he was an alcoholic as such but he certainly had a drink problem. He was never actually prosecuted for drink driving but he had a couple of alcohol-related incidents in his car. In one, he had a crash and ended up in a field somewhere, and in the other he refused to give a sample when stopped by the police and was banned from driving for a year.

In 2009, long after we'd ended our association with him, Derek was flying home from presiding over *Michael Jackson: The Live Séance* – a TV special for Sky, which was called a car crash of a different kind by some newspaper reviewers – and he made unwelcome headlines by shouting at a baby who was crying on the plane. His associate later put the blame on 'a small glass of wine' interacting badly with some cough medicine Derek had been taking. Well, maybe. But we'd seen Derek in too many drink-fuelled rages over the years to be entirely convinced by that explanation.

Our earliest clear evidence that something was amiss with Derek's psychic abilities came at Athelhampton Hall in Dorset during the filming of the first series.

'Oh, there's the ghost of a cooper in here, a barrel maker,' Derek exclaimed as we went into the cellar. He even went so far as to imitate the motions of a cooper hammering a barrel into shape.

Karl spoke to the owner of Athelhampton Hall before we left to make sure she was happy with everything we'd done, which is something he does at every location we visit.

'Actually, there is something I'm not comfortable with,' she said. 'What your medium said about there being a ghost of a cooper in the cellar … well, that was a story my dad made up for the brochure.'

So Derek had obviously read about this fictitious ghost, or someone had told him about it. Either way, that information had not come from a spiritual source.

Karl and I were understandably perturbed by this but were prepared to give Derek the benefit of the doubt. Karl took him aside to have a quiet word.

'Listen, mate,' he said. 'You mustn't panic if you don't pick anything up. Just be truthful and say there's nothing there if there isn't. It doesn't mean you're no good if nothing comes through. We'll still carry on with the investigation.'

Derek immediately complained to the channel about us for doing this, which was a shame because we absolutely weren't calling him a fake at this point. We just wanted to deal with it without any fuss and remind him quietly that Karl and I intended everything in the show to be real and not made up. We've said the same to every medium we've ever used on *Most Haunted*, not only to make them aware of our standards but also to make them feel relaxed and not under pressure.

And Derek, more than most, was someone who needed his fragile ego massaging. Indeed, as the show started gaining popularity, it inevitably attracted more attention and he would get terribly upset about some of the things that were being written about him on internet forums and by critics. He had an extremely thin skin.

Derek would get so wounded sometimes, in fact, that it would hold up the filming of the show, and Karl would spend hours just talking to him and calming him down to try to coax him back in front of the camera. Maybe that was a mistake. Perhaps we indulged him too much, but what else were we supposed to do?

Living TV certainly indulged him. Having told Karl and me to dump Derek after they saw the pilot – something that we really had to fight – they slowly but surely changed their minds once they saw how popular the show was becoming. They ended up usually backing Derek even when they knew things were becoming strained between us.

As far as Living was concerned, Derek was our problem. 'Deal with it. Deal with him,' they'd tell us whenever an issue arose.

And we did, as nicely and professionally as we could.

\* \* \*

# Chapter 9

Around the time of our third series, in 2003, Karl and I were summoned to a meeting with Derek, his associate and Living TV executives. The associate wasted no time in telling us that Derek wanted a 50 per cent share of our company, Antix, which he claimed we'd promised him when we hired him.

'I've made *Most Haunted* successful,' Derek said. 'So now I want half of it.'

I was gobsmacked. Not only was Derek's claim that we'd promised him anything totally untrue, but I couldn't believe his sense of entitlement and ingratitude.

It was less than three years since he begged us to be a part of the *Most Haunted* pilot because he knew his career would be falling apart without it; less than three years after we'd really had to fight to keep him when Living TV wanted us to ditch him and find another medium. Yet here he was now, demanding half of the company that Karl and I had risked every penny of our savings to create.

The channel bosses looked at us and suggested that maybe we *should* give him something, to which we responded icily that given they owned all the broadcast rights to *Most Haunted* maybe *they* should give Derek a share of Living TV instead. They weren't going to do that. Of course they weren't.

Karl and I were not prepared to give Derek any share in our company, so we got up to end the meeting. My inner Biddy Baxter came out and, seething inside, I said a terse goodbye before walking out. Karl remained just for a moment.

'I'd like to say thank you,' he told the channel. 'This obviously means the end of *Most Haunted* but it's been fun. If we have any other ideas, we'll bring them to you.'

Karl then looked at Derek's associate and Derek in turn. 'Fuck you. And fuck you very much.' He then left to join me outside the room.

The very last thing Living wanted was for *Most Haunted* to come to a premature end. We were their only hit. The only show keeping them afloat. One of the channel bosses ran out of the room to stop us before we left the building.

'Look, let's all calm down. Please don't go until I've talked to Derek.'

It took all of 20 minutes for Derek to back off.

'It's okay,' he said. 'I'll carry on. I don't want half of your company.'

'You weren't going to get it,' I said.

So we carried on making *Most Haunted* but I found it very hard after that because I was suddenly aware I was working with someone who'd wanted to take away half of what Karl and I had worked so hard for.

Up until then I'd thought of Derek as being a deeply spiritual man; kind and understanding and part of the team. Now he'd revealed himself to be just the opposite. It was so clear he wasn't the man I thought he was.

That was it for me. I just completely shut down where Derek was concerned. I always remained perfectly polite and was very professional when we were filming together. But we no longer sat together for lunch and so on.

The crew were also starting to keep their distance from Derek and his small entourage because of the disdainful way he treated them. They no longer knew where they stood with him and never knew quite what he'd do next. He was volatile and unpredictable. Everyone who worked on *Most Haunted* could see that fame had changed Derek, and not for the better. It felt like we'd created an egotistical nightmare.

By far the biggest problem for us, though, was Derek's credibility. As *Most Haunted* attracted bigger audiences, it also generated more press interest. But a lot of the press was negative, mostly because of Derek's possessions, which were becoming more prolific with each series. It got to the point where he was supposedly being possessed more than once in an episode. This puzzled us because many experts in the field told us that when a medium is possessed it can take a long time to get over it and some are completely drained for days afterwards. Derek seemed to be having too many to be plausible.

I have seen other mediums affected to the point where they've fainted or collapsed. When Brian Shepherd was badly affected I knew it was real; it really upset me. It was becoming increasingly clear that Derek's 'possessions' weren't the same. Brian is a good friend and I trust him completely; he and the American medium Patrick Mathews are the only ones I would ever work with now.

We took Derek aside to ask him what was going on. 'The bosses at the channel have told me that the possessions are the best thing in the show,' he explained. 'They say I am what makes *Most Haunted* and that the audience loves me and the possessions. So I'm gonna continue doing them if that's what they want.' That really alarmed us.

However, it was the information he was coming up with when supposedly possessed that worried us even more. On one occasion,

Derek claimed to have been possessed by the spirit of a Spitfire pilot, a specific person. He would come up with the facts that anyone could find out online, such as when the pilot was born and when he died, but he faltered when we started asking specific questions.

'How far can you fly in your Spitfire?' I asked.

'I'm not telling you. That is secret information,' Derek snapped.

'Where did you take off from? Where did you land? How high can you fly?' We asked technical questions that any Spitfire pilot would know but the 'possessed' Derek refused to answer and instead became angry.

'You impertinent person! How dare you ask me these questions?'

It was obvious deflection and we were very disappointed in him. Karl and I had always wanted *Most Haunted* to be honest and truthful. We still do. But now we realised we had someone we couldn't be sure about. Someone we thought might be faking at least *part* of what he was doing. When you put your trust in someone and they turn out not to be who they claimed to be, that's hugely disappointing. We had put our full trust in Derek and it felt like he'd betrayed us. Worse, he was betraying our audience.

Then things started to spiral out of control when Derek's 'possessions' became violent as his ego inflated. He also became increasingly absurd to the point that on one occasion he even claimed to be a unicorn on camera and proceeded to trot around. Our big worry was that members of the crew were starting to get hurt as 'possessed' Derek lashed out. He was also becoming very nasty verbally, especially towards me.

# Chapter 9

I don't know if he knew we suspected him of faking by this stage and was feeling paranoid, but he was really starting to take it out on me especially. On one occasion, he focused on me, stuck his nose almost in my face and spat out, 'You're a witch. You're a witch.' It was obvious he really hated me. Other times, he'd say explicitly sexual things to me when he was supposedly possessed.

'I love your breasts,' he said. 'You're gonna show me your breasts. C'mon, show me your breasts.'

Some of the things he said about me were extremely vile and twisted, and we had to cut them out in the edits entirely. His behaviour was so weird and unsettling that our then-resident parapsychologist, who also worked in psychiatry, told me: 'There's definitely something not right there, at all.'

However, no matter what he did, the channel always backed Derek when we told them of his deteriorating behaviour. And to the public, Derek maintained his saintly persona. Hands always clasped, as if in saintly prayer, he would humbly bless them and thank them for coming. They'd go away thinking he was lovely.

One crunch moment came in 2004 during the production of *Most Haunted Live* in Stratford. There were about 100 of us who were working on the show in a bar and Derek was sitting on a sofa next to the presenter of that live show. Derek turned to him and said, 'There's a spirit here for you. I want to do a reading.'

The presenter was talking to someone else and didn't want to be interrupted and said something like 'In a minute, Derek.'

Derek didn't like that and made a grab for him, ripping his shirt. The presenter was bewildered as Derek suddenly then went into full 'possession' mode, screaming and rolling around on the floor. It was awful to watch and very upsetting for those who hadn't seen Derek acting like that before.

Karl and a couple of security guards had to pin Derek down to keep him calm before escorting him to his hotel room, where his wife took over to look after him.

Early on, I spoke to one executive of my concern that Derek might be faking some things and that some of his information might not be coming from a spiritual source. But they believed Derek and were keen for us to keep working with him. We had reached the stage when we really didn't have much appetite to continue making *Most Haunted* for the channel while they continued to back Derek, who I feared could be threatening our integrity.

Things had become so bad that I wasn't speaking to Derek at all, except on camera. Our relationship had broken down completely because I had no respect for him whatsoever and anyone watching those last few shows Derek made with us can see that I'm unable to disguise the contempt I was feeling for what he was saying. Frankly, I didn't believe a word that was coming out of his mouth. Also, by this time, the crew really disliked Derek. It was sad given that everyone on the team, not just Karl and me, had been so supportive of him in the beginning.

When we were making *Most Haunted USA*, Derek travelled separately from the rest of us and arrived very late one night. Karl and I were awoken by a call from the night manager at the hotel where we were all staying.

'I want you all to leave my hotel now,' he told us. 'I will not have my staff spoken to in that way.'

'Who's been rude?' we asked, perplexed.

'Your psychic guy.'

'Look,' I said. 'If he's the one who's been rude, he's the one you should kick out.'

We eventually managed to smooth things over enough so the manager reluctantly let us stay.

Derek started saying he needed the toilet a lot when we were doing the walkabouts in the show. It was every 10 or 15 minutes sometimes. He blamed the toll the spirits were taking on his body, but some of the crew members became suspicious about this.

Obviously, everyone needs a toilet break occasionally on a shoot, but the audience at home never sees it because we edit round it. It's standard practice to turn their microphones off when they attend a call of nature, but one of the sound guys decided to let Derek's mic keep running on one occasion to see if he really was up to anything.

'I think you need to hear this,' he told us afterwards.

When he played back the recording he'd made, we could hear Derek on his phone in the toilet cubicle.

'Can you tell me about the history of this place?' he asked whoever was on the other end of his phone. 'And what's the story about the dead children?'

That was infuriating because we'd always made a point of never telling Derek where we were investigating beforehand. We did learn later, however, that he knew from the channel where we were going next.

The crew also got wind that if they said anything within earshot of Derek's entourage it would be fed back to him and often come out in an investigation as if from the spirit world. To test this out, we dropped in some rubbish about copies of the Bible having been written at Ordsall Hall in Salford. Sure enough, as we walked around the location he claimed he could sense the monks writing the Bible. At other times he'd come up with names we knew were made up.

We knew there was no way we could carry on like this but, as it turned out, everything came to a head before we'd even finished shooting series six. We were filming at Arreton Manor on the Isle of Wight when Derek went into yet another alleged possession. He attacked the make-up artist, really frightening her. Then he started lashing out and punching people, all while being supposedly possessed, of course. It was terrible to witness.

It was also the final straw as far as all the crew were concerned.

The following morning, they came to our hotel room because they'd snapped. Enough was enough. They told us they would refuse to work on any future episodes of *Most Haunted* that Derek was involved in.

Who could blame them? They were fearing for their own safety, which was perfectly understandable. *Most Haunted* is an unusual programme to work on as it is, but then to work alongside someone so unpredictable, someone who could be talking normally one minute then trying to hurt a make-up artist or punch a cameraman the next, was unacceptable. We asked them to put it in an email to us.

## Chapter 9

When their email arrived, we forwarded it to the channel, who told us that each of the crew would have to email us with individual specific and detailed experiences and complaints. They did and we forwarded their emails along with one of our own, saying that we didn't want to work with Derek if our hard-working crew wouldn't.

After reading all the emails and realising how serious this was, the channel decided they had to do something about Derek.

'It's okay. Leave it with us. You won't have to work with Derek any more.'

What they did was give Derek his own show called *Derek Acorah's Ghost Towns*. He was never told about the emails from the crew and believed he was being given his own show by the channel because he'd been the most important part of *Most Haunted*.

I strongly believed it was wrong of them to give Derek his own show when they knew of our concerns that he had faked so much, but at least it got him off our backs, and for that I was grateful.

Our viewing figures went through the roof after Derek left, whereas the numbers for his new show were terrible. *Ghost Towns* really bombed. That proved to us how the audiences were feeling about Derek's later years on *Most Haunted*. I'm sure that they, like us, had thought when he went into yet another of his 'possessions', *Oh, hang on a minute, now, this is getting too far-fetched for words.*

Audiences aren't stupid. They can see when someone is faking it when they're watching TV.

I think the failure of his new show coupled with our great success with the American episodes led to some bitterness festering inside Derek, and my last direct and bizarre contact with him, if indeed it *was* him, might have been triggered by that.

While we were doing one of the US live shows, someone left a voice message for me. It wasn't a death threat as such but it was still very threatening.

'I'm watching you and I'm coming to get you.' The voice was disguised and the accent was a weird mix of half-scouse/half-cod American.

The producers at the Discovery Channel were shocked and appalled when they heard it, and they insisted we needed to get it investigated because they didn't know if the call was made in the US or not, or how serious the threat against me might be.

I handed my phone over to the police, who in turn contacted the police in the UK. The British police traced the call back to an address near Liverpool and, well, I think we all drew our own conclusions but I chose to take no further action.

After that, the only times I ever heard from Derek were indirectly through the press when he would periodically slag me off. His television career was practically over by this stage and he was just doing bits and bobs here and there.

Derek said some terrible things about me there. Really nasty and hurtful stuff. Things that I really didn't deserve. And he only ever said them about me, no other member of the team. Your natural reaction when you read that kind of stuff is to retaliate and to say none of it is true. I really resented the fact he could say all these things about me publicly but I always forced myself to keep my counsel and not respond. Apart from Karl and my kids, no one really knew how upset I was about what Derek was saying about me because I've never really talked about it until now.

There was, however, one incident when he said something that Karl and I thought we simply couldn't let him get away with. We felt we had to sue for defamation. It was so outrageous that our lawyer told us the case was cut and dried, and there was no doubt we would win.

He also had a word of caution, however: 'You made Derek a star but no one knows who he is any more. If you pursue this, it'll put him back on the front pages of the newspapers and reinvigorate his career. If that's what you want, fine, let's go ahead. Personally, I'd let it go. It's going to cost you hundreds of thousands to bring the case and even when you win you're not going to get your money back. All you're likely to do is to make him famous again.'

He was right, of course. So, after Derek received a strongly worded letter from our lawyers, he said he would never repeat those statements again.

\* \* \*

When Derek died in January 2020 at the age of 69, Karl and I put out a brief statement: 'Our condolences are with Derek's family at this time.' Some newspapers took me to task for that, suggesting it had been too curt. However, they'd no idea of the hell he'd put us and all the *Most Haunted* crew through for years. Derek could have brought everything Karl and I had worked for and invested in crashing down. Our integrity might have been trashed forever.

In fact, the *Daily Mirror* had run a big piece about *Most Haunted* being faked, but it was Derek's fakery they were reporting on, not ours. So while we obviously couldn't have let his passing go without comment, to have said more would have been hypocritical.

When I think back now to the *Most Haunted* shows we made with Derek, my overwhelming feeling about him is one of sadness. I don't think he could handle seeing the new heights the show went to after he'd left. Derek had always craved success in America, so seeing how well *Most Haunted* was received there without him must have been a terribly bitter pill for him to swallow.

Even so, despite all the crap he threw at us, if Derek was still alive and came up to me and said, 'Oh, Yvie, I'm sorry for everything I put you and Karl through,' I'd give him the biggest hug and tell him we could move on. I've cried many times over the years when I've thought about what Derek did to us, and I can still feel bloody angry about him trying to steal half our business. But if he were here now and owned up to his bad behaviour, I would forgive him.

The one thing Derek craved above all else was to be hailed as the greatest psychic in the world. He ensured that didn't happen all by himself. He was the architect of his own downfall and that makes him a tragic figure in my book. If he'd just worked on developing the psychic ability he had – and despite all the obvious fakery, I do still like to believe he had a tiny bit – he could have continued the *Most Haunted* journey with us. Everyone on the team was behind him in the beginning; Karl and me more than anyone. Without us fighting for him he wouldn't have been on the show in the first place.

However, I do also blame the channel, as well as the adoring acolytes he surrounded himself with, for a lot of what happened. I wish the channel had taken our initial concerns more seriously and perhaps together we could have stopped this unravelling. But they believed Derek and backed him. We wanted to tell Derek to wind his neck in, to keep it real and to enjoy the ride. It's been a great ride and it would have been lovely to have had him on it with us.

Instead, Living's support fed his ego. An ego that gave way to bitterness and led ultimately to the melancholy twilight of his final years.

All of this had severely damaged our trust in Living TV, and even though *Most Haunted* would go from strength to strength, the relationship with the channel was now dead in the water.

It was time to work with some new faces.

*Chapter 10*

---

# DEATH IN
# VENICE

*O*NCE DEREK HAD LEFT *Most Haunted*, it was like we'd been liberated. The show was fresher and we felt able to be more adventurous with the format, to push our limits as producers and investigators. We were reinvigorated and I felt our shows were better than ever. But sadly, our relationship with Living was worsening. We were grateful that they'd thrown us a lifeline back in 2001 when no one else would, of course, but the more successful *Most Haunted* became, the more pressure they put on us to deliver episodes. We'd become crucial to their very survival. But we felt that we weren't being given the editorial freedom that our success warranted. In fact, it's hard to describe just how bad our relationship with the executives was then. The more we did for them, the worse it seemed to get.

So when the opportunity for a completely new show arose in 2006, we decided to take it elsewhere.

I was appearing on *Never Mind the Buzzcocks* at the BBC studios in Wood Lane and there was a knock on my dressing-room door. When Karl answered it, I was gobsmacked to see Robbie Williams framed in the doorway.

Coming in, he told us: 'I'm such a massive fan of you guys. I'm really into ghosts and UFOs and all that kind of stuff. I'd love to come on *Most Haunted*.'

We were thrilled. Of course Robbie Williams could come on our show. But then the idea developed into a separate show that would be called 'Ghost Hunting with Yvette and Robbie'. He was a huge star and if that's how he wanted to do it only an idiot would say no.

We decided we'd take 'Ghost Hunting with Yvette and Robbie' to ITV2. We didn't feel bad about this; we'd already floated the idea of a celebrity ghost-hunting show with Living and they'd turned it down.

When we took the idea to ITV, we just had to mention the words 'Robbie Williams' and they said, 'We'll have it!'

The show was commissioned instantly but then Robbie's record company told him he couldn't do it because there had been a backlash in the press to a radio interview he'd done in which he'd stated that he believes in UFOs. They felt that if he did anything else related to the paranormal it might harm his career.

We called ITV2 and told them we'd lost Robbie.

'That's not a problem,' they said. 'We've already booked the time slot so just give us someone else.'

We approached Girls Aloud and, somewhat to our surprise, they said yes and it was broadcast a couple of weeks before Christmas in 2006.

That was only supposed to be a one-off show as we were still fully committed to making *Most Haunted* for Living. However, the day after the Girls Aloud show went out, I had just filled my car with fuel at the service station and was about to drive home when my phone rang.

It was ITV2.

'Yvette, we've had the overnights in for the show. We got just under a million. Oh my God, it's amazing.'

Those were spectacular numbers for ITV2, so I could understand their excitement.

'Can you do us another one?' they asked.

That was how *Ghost Hunting with...* began.

Some of the most memorable times on the show were when Boyzone and Louis Walsh were on the show. They were a bit cocky when they arrived at the notorious Edinburgh Vaults.

'This is a load of rubbish,' one of the band members said.

'It's a TV show, so which one of you is gonna be chucking stuff?' said another.

'No, it's real,' I insisted.

'What a load of rubbish.'

These big strong lads weren't quite so cocky when it all started kicking off. In fact, we had one wonderful shot of Louis Walsh clutching his pearls and trotting like a pony as he screamed, 'That's enough now, let's stop!'

The band's Keith Duffy asked me if I used anything for protection while I was investigating the paranormal.

'I do,' I said, showing him the tiny heart-shaped pendant on my necklace. 'I have the ashes of my father in here.'

'Tiny man, was he?' Keith joked.

That made me fall about laughing, so now I say I have *some* of my dad's ashes in my pendant. And although I say they protect me, it's mainly a comfort to know part of him is there close to me.

By the end of the investigation, they were all intrigued by what they'd witnessed, especially poor Stephen Gately, who was really bowled over by it all. Even when it got to four in the morning he wanted to keep going.

'We need to wrap,' I said.

'No. I want to see more. Let's stay a bit longer.'

Stephen sadly died of a heart condition just six weeks after the show was televised in summer 2009. It was his final TV appearance.

I was pleasantly surprised by the Happy Mondays. In fact, if pushed I would have to nominate them as the funniest and best of all the celebrities we worked with on that series. They were a great bunch of people and all so up for doing the show. Shaun Ryder couldn't get enough of it. Even when we'd filmed all through the night and we'd got to around 5am, they were begging us to keep going, just like Stephen Gately, because they were loving it so much.

We were filming at an old prison in Lincoln and at one point I had to lock Shaun into a haunted prison cell. As he sat down on a chair, one of the production crew took me aside.

'Yvette,' he said. 'Whatever you do, only pretend to lock him in because the lock is dodgy and might jam.'

Of course, I'd forgotten every word about this when I came to do it for the camera and I locked Shaun in properly. The result is some of the funniest footage we've ever captured as we had a locked-off camera in the cell. Shaun was screaming and chuntering to himself as he paced the cell. And then he shouted some more.

We eventually found a second key and unlocked the door.

'Something's burned me leg!' he shouted. 'It's burned me leg!'

'Take your trousers down,' I instructed. 'Let's take a look at it.'

Next there's a shot of Shaun Ryder with his trousers round his ankles and me on my knees looking for burn marks on his thighs because he was convinced that someone, or something, had stubbed out a cigarette on his leg.

Shaun's bandmate Bez almost became aggressive in a room on his own as it suddenly dawned on him that everything he was experiencing wasn't the result of someone playing tricks on him, while Julie Gordon, the backing singer, collapsed and went catatonic when we conducted a Ouija board session.

That show started out all light and funny, and it was amazing watching their faces change as things started to take a darker and more sinister turn and they realised it was all for real. But they loved it and Shaun even egged me on to do my ancient Kabbalah chanting that I sometimes use to get activity going. I love that chant because it originated in Homs, in Syria, where my grandmother was from. It has the same effect as a Tibetan singing bowl, so the tone resonates through the atmosphere. It's amazing; whenever I use it on an investigation, poltergeist activity starts up as soon as I've finished the last word.

'Do that fucking chanting,' Shaun kept saying. 'It gets it all going.'

That was such a fun episode to make and, in fact, most of the celebrities we had on *Ghost Hunting with...* were good sports. We did have a couple of divas and I really lost my temper with one of them. They thought they were marvellous and better than everyone else, whereas in fact they were just plain rude. When one of our experts was doing his piece to camera explaining the history of the place and who'd died there, they just started laughing at him and chatting away to their mates. I wondered who the hell they thought they were and I tore into them because I won't tolerate diva-ish behaviour like that from anyone, especially as they were being paid £35,000 for a few hours' work. In fact, Karl and I hadn't wanted to use them at all because we didn't want to pay their ridiculous fee. ITV2 were keen to have them on the show, though, and they stumped up the money.

'Just pack it in,' I snapped at them. 'You're being incredibly disrespectful. Who do you think you are? You're no better than anyone else here.'

I really cannot stand unprofessional behaviour like that but you sadly find it all the way through our industry, not least among executives.

And I've met quite a few of those in my time.

\* \* \*

We made 12 editions of *Ghost Hunting with...* across five years and it was a huge success for the channel. Some editions of the show made the top slot in ITV2's ratings and we were never out of their top-ten programmes. They would often use our shows as a spike to prop up other shows as we got such good numbers.

But Living TV weren't at all happy with us doing a full series and insisted on a lot of restrictions. I wasn't allowed to wear the same clothes as I did on *Most Haunted*. I wasn't even allowed to use the same make-up lady.

It wasn't long before they were also asking us for spin-off shows of their own. I remember taking a call from them in 2007. 'We need something for the summer,' they said. '*Most Haunted* fans love the show, but the channel is getting crap viewing figures in July and August so we need to put on something *Most Haunted*-related then.'

Karl and I came up with *Most Haunted: Midsummer Murders*, which was a spin on the original series *Midsomer Murders* in that we investigated unsolved murders through the prism of paranormal investigation. We only made one series of that and sometimes even I forget about it completely.

We also produced a series called *In Bed with Yvette and Karl*, which was essentially a reality show where viewers could watch Karl and me pratting about at home. That was just another programme to boost Living TV's viewing figures but, again, it demonstrated how important we and *Most Haunted* had become to them.

Karl and I still had to keep reassuring Living TV that *Ghost Hunting with...* was a completely different beast from *Most Haunted* and we worked hard to put clear blue water between the two shows. I drove around locations in a black taxi for one thing but the biggest difference was that it was all about the celebrities, not me.

It turns out that many of them were huge fans of *Most Haunted* already. I remember an incident the morning after we'd done a *Most Haunted Live* broadcast from the Churchill War Rooms in London. That was another of my favourite lives because it was such a privilege to be allowed to broadcast from there, and from parts of the building that are usually no-go areas. I was also in my element because of my love for anything to do with the military and the Second World War. We recorded some remarkable paranormal activity in the War Rooms, not least telephones ringing when no one was there. Telephones that weren't even connected.

The morning afterwards, I was busy doing an interview while Karl left the hotel to go and fetch the car. He was stopped by a woman, who had jumped out of a pub to intercept him.

'Oh my God, oh my God, it's you, isn't it?'

'Hello, yes,' he said. 'Do I know you?'

'No,' she said. 'But me and my husband are huge fans of *Most Haunted*. We were watching the show last night and it was fantastic. We were so scared that we had to keep the lights on all night after we went to bed. Will you talk to him if I put him on the phone now?'

Being polite as he always is, Karl said that of course he would and she passed her phone to him.

'Hello,' he said. 'It's Karl from *Most Haunted*.'

The man at the other end said in a broad northern accent. 'We loved your show last night. We thought it was great.'

Like me, Karl always takes an interest in our fans and so he asked, 'What do you do?'

'Oh, well, I'm an actor.'

'That's interesting,' Karl said. 'Are you doing anything at the moment?'

'Yeah,' the man said. 'I'm on set now. We're just on a break.'

'Would I know you from anything?' Karl asked.

'Possibly,' the man said. 'It's Sean Bean here.'

That was such a great moment for us.

\* \* \*

Perhaps one of our biggest fans was one of my greatest friends. Paul O'Grady and I had always got on well and, as we were fellow northerners, we shared the same sense of humour (I'm certain that growing up in the north and being northern gave me the sense of humour I have). He'd always had an interest in the paranormal and after I'd appeared as a guest on *The Paul O'Grady Show* once he told me he'd love to appear in a *Most Haunted* episode. How could I say no? It turned out not to be a one-off as we loved him joining us on the investigation team. He gave us some of our most memorable moments. On one *Most Haunted Live* show in 2005, which focused on Jack the Ripper and the East End, viewers saw how Paul left me to fend for myself in a cellar beneath the Blind Beggar pub in London when activity kicked off.

What was so funny about that was Paul always said to me before an investigation, 'You'll be all right with me, Yvette. Don't you worry. I'll look after you.' Then he was the first one to bolt when anything happened.

'Don't leave me! Don't leave me in here on my own!' I screamed in that cellar as he bolted for the exit after he was convinced he'd seen something uncanny lurching out of the darkness at us.

'I'm getting my bloody arse out of here,' he cried.

'What is it, Paul? What've you seen?'

'Over here, where the ale comes in,' he said, pointing at a corner in the gloom. 'I'm serious. I'm not taking the piss. There. Right there. Something was there. I'm telling you now. On my life, it was there. I'm serious.'

'What did you hear?' I asked.

'I didn't *hear* anything,' he said.

# Chapter 10

'You mean you saw it?'

'Yes. I'll show you what it looked like. I'll do it for you now. It looked like something was coming out of here slowly.' And he acted out the movements of what he had seen coming out of the corner.

It looked very funny to watch on TV, but it's even funnier when you know that the man who swore to always protect me was the one legging it out of the door first. It became a bit of a running gag between us every time we got together.

In one *Ghost Hunting with...* episode, I took Paul, Natasha Hamilton from Atomic Kitten, and actors Jennifer Ellison and Philip Olivier to Palermo, Sicily. There, we were horrified by visiting the Capuchin Catacombs where hundreds of decomposed corpses stand or lie completely exposed: the oldest corpse dates to 1599. It's a rather macabre tourist attraction these days where you can pay to literally stare death in the face. We were all deeply affected by the corpse of an almost two-year-old child, Rosalia Lombardo, who was put into a glass coffin in 1920 and is perfectly preserved. One of the last corpses to be placed in the catacombs, she genuinely looks like she's sleeping. But was she at rest?

Well, we certainly believed we contacted the spirit of little Rosalia and her playfulness was evident when Paul was convinced she'd untied the belt on his jacket. Jennifer felt we were intruding on the dignity of the dead and it was hard not to feel the same. I was particularly affected by seeing the corpses of little Rosalia and all the other children. It wasn't a nice location at all.

Undeterred, Paul agreed to return to Italy with me for a new series that Living had commissioned: *Death in Venice*, which we announced on his ITV show in May 2009.

We'd be heading to the forbidding island of Poveglia in the Venetian Lagoon. The island is a place that couldn't be more different from the tourist trap of St Mark's Square, just a stone's throw away across the water to the southwest. Not that tourists would know how desolate it is because visits to Poveglia are usually prohibited. Maybe that's because the island is claimed by some to be one of the most haunted places on Earth. Our investigation would prove to be one of the most memorably bizarre episodes I've ever been involved in.

The island of Poveglia has a horrific past and reputation. There was once a mental asylum standing there, and during the plague they used to take all the bodies over there and dump them in the water or on the island. It was also a place of quarantine, where the infected were left to die. We were given special permission to film on the island and I remember thinking on arrival that the sand was so lovely. That was until I realised it wasn't sand. It was ashes from the bodies they burned. The ones they didn't dump at sea, that is.

Bodies of vampires were also found on the island. Or, at least, the bodies of what people during the plague years *believed* to be vampires, according to local legend. So it's no wonder that the island is reputed to be haunted by ghosts and vampires and all kinds of horrendous things. The perfect place for a paranormal investigation, you might think.

We were on the deck of a small fishing boat, somewhere between Venice itself and Poveglia. It was well after 11pm but not yet quite midnight. The night was still warm but the darkness was only punctured by lights coming from Venice itself.

## Chapter 10

The beautiful ancient city centre had long since emptied of tourists, and those who hadn't been shipped back to nearby resorts along the coast were probably finishing off the remnants of a fine meal or taking a last stroll along the streets and over the fabled bridges.

Paul and I were sitting opposite each other at a small table on the boat. To this day, local fishermen trawl up skeletons and bones around the shores of Poveglia, so we had the idea to try to contact the souls of those who'd been unceremoniously dumped in the sea simply because they had the plague. Where better to do that than out in the lagoon itself?

On the table between us there was a Ouija board to help us contact the dead.

The other people onboard comprised a small camera crew, an Italian interpreter and the local boat owner. You could tell the two Italians thought we were mad just from the looks they'd been giving us ever since we set sail.

But then it started.

'What the fuck?'

I'm not quite sure now if it was Paul or myself who uttered the expletive under our breath first because Paul was no stranger to a choice word. But regular viewers of *Most Haunted* will know it could very easily have been me.

What had triggered it was knocking.

I was well used to spirits using knocks to communicate by now, of course, but this was a new one even for me because this knocking was coming from *underneath* the boat. From something in the water beneath us. Which was not what we expected.

Suddenly, the two Italians weren't quite so dismissive of us. Now they were scared.

Paul and I looked at each other, trying to make sense of this. As we listened for more knocks, trying to encourage whoever was making them, we were suddenly bathed in a searing white light. But this was nothing supernatural. It was a searchlight accompanied by the sound of a high-powered police launch closing in on us rapidly.

The police had spotted us and were coming to find out just what we were up to.

I looked at Paul again and then at the Ouija board. We weren't doing anything wrong. Were we? As the police launch approached determinedly, it was clear we'd find out soon enough. And that this might take some explaining if they suspected we were drug smugglers or gun runners.

As the police launch drew level with the fishing boat, we feared the investigation might end before it had properly begun.

'What should we do?' Paul and I hissed to each other from the corner of our mouths, both swearing like troopers.

Should we try to hide the Ouija board, which was sitting there openly in the centre of the table? But what would be the point? There was nowhere to put it, and if we tried to hide it that might look even more suspicious. So we did nothing and waited to see how things played out.

One of the Italian policemen shouted across, demanding to know what we were doing. Our interpreter called back that we were making a TV programme.

'What kind of programme?' they asked.

'A documentary. About ghosts.'

The policeman looked at us again. Then he just smiled and told us to carry on.

Our fear of arrest receded as quickly as the police launch did. But the knocking had intensified in the meantime. This was a soul – or souls – who very much wanted to be in touch.

I asked whoever it was to knock once for every one of them who was present. And suddenly the knocking sounded like a machine-gun.

Rat-a-tat-tat!

There must've been hundreds of spirits getting in touch with us. And, trust me, you've never seen a grown man spooked as much as Paul was. But then everyone aboard that fishing boat was spooked by what was happening. Me included.

We asked the spirits if they were at peace, or did they need our help to move on? They didn't. All they wanted to do was to let us know they were there and to confirm that the stories about what had happened to them were true.

The location, the bizarre events and being with Paul all made that investigation so memorable for me. He was a good friend and always backed *Most Haunted*. Whenever he was asked to go on other paranormal programmes he always refused because he believed in and loved what we were doing.

'No. If I'm doing it, I'm only gonna do it with Yvette again,' he'd reply.

He dug up a witch's bottle in his garden once and freaked out. They're not uncommon to find in the walls or gardens of old properties; they've usually got a wax seal and have strands of human hair or nails in them, and are intended as a protection against evil witchcraft. Paul wasn't happy when I told him what it was, so I had to reassure him that a witch's bottle was usually used for good. We're conditioned by evil witch movies to think of the classic old hag in a pointed hat on a broomstick and feel unsettled when we hear about witchcraft, but most witches were just herbalists.

Karl and I went one better after we found a mummified cat under the floorboards in our new house shortly after moving in. We think it's about 400 years old and was probably something to do with witchcraft. We now keep it under the bath because bad things seemed to happen when we removed it from the house: the atmosphere was awful; Karl and I felt fed up; and the kids were arguing constantly. When we brought the cat back in, all was well again.

In March 2023, I was numb all day when I heard Paul had died. Then, that night I was watching something on the computer and Karl asked if I was okay. That was it. I broke down and couldn't stop crying.

I've saved all of Paul's messages on my answering machine. It feels weird that he'll not call again because he'd often ring up and say, 'Hi, Yvette, I'm just here filming …' and then proceed to tell me all about whatever he was working on. He would send me a text every Halloween to wish us luck, and to say how jealous he was of us and wished he was coming on whatever investigation we were doing that night.

Shortly after the first investigation Paul did with us in the East End of London, he was due to join us on a week of live shows in Transylvania. Sadly, he had a heart attack before we flew out and couldn't come. His health didn't stop him joining us on later shows but it eventually took him from us far too soon. I was privileged to know him and will always miss him. He was a beautiful man and a true friend.

\* \* \*

After five years of making hugely enjoyable *Ghost Hunting with...* shows, the three executives at ITV2 who loved and supported our work had all moved on to other shows and we then had to deal with others who replaced them. The channel now made their disdain for the show obvious and turned down every idea for potential guests that we submitted.

'The Sex Pistols with John Lydon have agreed to do the show,' we told them.

'No, I don't think so.'

'Well, how about the Osbournes? We've got them.'

'No.'

'Why not?' we asked.

'Nobody knows who those people are any longer,' they said.

'Are you mad?' we asked. 'Of course everyone knows who the Sex Pistols and the Osbournes are.'

Shortly after that, all the surviving cast members of *The A-Team* agreed to do the show. Mr T spoke to Karl on the phone and he said, 'I'll do it. But I ain't goin' in no haunted house on my own!'

We felt sure they'd commission this one. This was *The A-Team*, for goodness' sake! But it was another no.

'Give us a new list,' they'd say. 'Bring us new talent.'

So we did and every time they'd turn those down as well. It was clear to us that they were just going through the motions and we guessed they wouldn't commission any new episodes but didn't have the guts to tell us directly. In the end, the phone went dead and no one from ITV2 would call us back.

That was the end of *Ghost Hunting with…* A show that a lot of people enjoyed had died simply because a couple of executives hated it.

That was also the end of any interest ITV had in us or any kind of paranormal broadcasting.

It was not, however, my last association with a celebrity-driven ITV show as I took part in one of the most infamous years of *I'm a Celebrity … Get Me Out of Here* in 2015. My time on the show came about when I attended the *TV Choice* Awards and found I was on the same table as one of its celebrity bookers. He asked if I would be interested in taking part in the next series.

'They've asked me before,' I said. 'And I've always turned it down because I'm not into eating bugs and all that kind of stuff.'

'I think you'd be really good at it,' he said.

I'd been craving adventure since hitting the menopause when I was about 46 or 47.

I must admit that I clutched my pearls when the doctor diagnosed me because I thought it was very premature as I wasn't yet 50.

And it was horrendous for a while. No one warned me that it would make my joints, ankles and hips hurt so much. Just watching me get out of bed every morning was a comedy routine in itself. But eventually I came to approach it positively.

'This is your time, now,' I told myself. 'The kids are grown up and it's time to do all those things that Karl and I have dreamed of doing. We can do them all now.'

One of those things was an urge to go adventuring around the world and I said to Karl at one point, 'Can we go to Africa? I went with *Blue Peter* years ago but I'd really like to go back and see it with you. Let's have an adventure and go on safari in Africa.'

He was up for that so we booked it and were all ready to go when we received an email from the Foreign Office. The area we were heading to was now on high alert because terrorists had been kidnapping Western tourists. The adventure suddenly didn't seem quite so appealing.

I looked at Karl and said, 'I really don't fancy being kidnapped, do you?'

'Not really,' he admitted.

So we binned the holiday, but I was still desperate to experience something new. *I'm a Celebrity* ... would certainly provide it. So I relented and told ITV I would do it.

For 18 long days in the jungle I often wished I hadn't because, while I had some great times in there, I had some bloody miserable ones as well.

One of the problems was boredom. Boredom and hunger. You sit around for hours on that show doing bugger all, and they keep you hungry. It's a deliberate tactic because once the lack of sugar kicks in, you start getting cranky and slagging each other off.

On the first day they wanted me to parachute into the camp, but I remembered Janet Ellis breaking her pelvis doing a parachute jump for *Blue Peter*.

'There is no way I'm parachuting in,' I told them. 'I'll go on a bareback camel ride if I have to get there but there is no way I'm jumping out of an aircraft.'

In the end, we were taken to the middle of the jungle and had to hike the rest of the way. It took us about a day to reach the camp.

When I had my preliminary chat with the production team, they asked if I was okay eating beans and rice.

'Yes,' I said. 'And will there be tea?'

'Oh yes,' they reassured me.

The production team had bananas, bottled water and those little energy snacks when we trekked to the camp, and whenever I got hungry they'd give me one of the bars.

*Oh, I'll be fine*, I thought, *they* do *give you snacks*.

I was a lamb to the slaughter because when I got to the camp, I discovered there were to be no more bananas, no more water, no more energy snacks. And definitely no tea.

They'd been fibbing.

Now, for someone who owned a teashop in Manchester at the time, going from having quite high levels of caffeine in my body to nothing at all was like going cold turkey. Add to that the symptoms of the menopause and let's say I wasn't in the best of places.

There *were* things to eat and drink, of course. For instance, on one occasion the gorgeous actress Jorgie Porter and I had to drink a milkshake containing crushed tarantulas for one of our tasks. Once that was completed, the first thing we did was to stick fingers down our throats to make ourselves sick. I could feel the hairs from the tarantulas' legs every time I swallowed for days afterwards.

# Chapter 10

Of course, you have a good idea what you're signing up for on that show and that you'll likely as not end up eating bugs and dealing with rats. But what I wasn't prepared for was one toxic contestant who was such a disagreeable and negative battleaxe that I cannot bring myself to utter or even write her name even to this day.

This person made that whole experience deeply unpleasant for me so, of course, the production team who match up all the challenges kept putting me with her to do them because they imagined the friction between us made for good telly. Every time I wanted to try to accomplish a challenge and to show that I could achieve something, she'd resolutely refuse to take part.

'No, I'm not doing that,' she'd sneer in a disdainful drawling accent.

I tried to keep calm for days but I eventually lost my temper with her after she'd been making some disgusting, deeply personal comments about me, Duncan Bannatyne, Tony Hadley and Brian Friedman.

'Just shut up,' I barked. 'You're getting on everyone's nerves.'

I believe #YesYvette was the number-one trending topic on social media that night but what really irked me was the way ITV edited the footage. The viewers at home only saw a little of just how vile she'd been to us all. We'd been sitting there for ages listening to her insults, taking it and taking it until I was the one who said that was enough now. I told her to her face what everyone else was saying about her behind her back. To be honest, I now wish I'd gone even further.

I've been in television long enough to know that producers deliberately introduce a provocative figure like her into a show to manufacture drama and create 'situations', and then use judicious editing to fit the narrative. When you're being kept hungry and given disgusting tasks to do, tempers are bound to get frayed. That's what the producers want and I get that. However, there is absolutely no excuse for anyone to be rude about someone's personal life the way she was.

That woman really spoiled the whole experience for me, which I regret because I bonded with all the other campmates, especially Duncan, who is the sweetest man. Some of the camp-mates wanted to tackle her about her toxic behaviour directly after the show ended, but Karl stepped in and persuaded them it would only fuel her notoriety further. It's such a shame because the year before all the contestants got on so well that it was prac-tically a love-in, and I'm sure I would have enjoyed it more if she hadn't been involved. As it was, I disliked her intensely and I never want to lay my eyes on her again.

I was the third celebrity to be voted off that year and I don't think I've ever felt a greater sense of relief when I walked across the bridge out of the camp. It was the longest I'd been away from Karl in 16 years and it was only by thinking about him and my kids that I got through that whole show. I couldn't help but feel emotional when I saw Karl waiting for me on the other side.

I think that really proves what a home bird I've become as I've got older. Years ago, I might have been tempted to do *Strictly Come Dancing* if they had asked but I don't think I would now. I wouldn't want to be in London away from Karl and my home for weeks on end.

## Chapter 10

In any case, I'm not sure I'm fit enough. I'd probably die on the first day of training. And while I've faced some of the most malevolent entities the paranormal can throw at me, I'm also not sure I want to face those judges.

I'm just happier working with the dead, even when they turn nasty!

## Chapter 11

# THE EVIL DEAD

*W*HEN I EMBARKED ON MY PARANORMAL JOURNEY in 2001, I was committed to finding out for myself if ghosts really existed. As I've always said, seeing is believing and I wanted to see and experience it for myself. But I must admit that I went into it with the rather naive belief, one that many people share, that while ghosts can frighten you, they can't harm you physically.

I was quite wrong.

In 2004 we investigated the Ancient Ram Inn in Wotton-under-Edge in Gloucestershire.

Thought to have been built on the site of devil worship and witchcraft, its history can be traced back centuries and it's said to be one of the most haunted pubs in the UK, with ghosts ranging from an evil incubus to a baby.

We'd all felt unsettled throughout the whole of that investigation, but things became far more sinister towards the end when something targeted Stuart.

'I'll be quite honest,' Stuart said as we walked around with night-vision cameras. 'In all the years we've been doing *Most Haunted*, I've never known a place like this.'

A little later, he said he was compelled to look at a particular area. 'I don't know why and it could be my imagination, but I've been drawn to look at that spot for the last two or three minutes.'

Stuart then complained of feeling dizzy and light-headed. 'I don't know what the hell it is,' he said, 'and I'm not lying or playing up for the camera, but I can feel something here.'

Suddenly, something unseen attacked Stuart in the dark, leaving him poleaxed on the floor, confused and bewildered about where he was, and crying out in distress and pain.

Karl immediately leapt into action, galvanising the team to help.

'Turn the torch on somebody! It's okay, Stu. I'm here. We've got you. Let's get you out of here.'

'I can't move,' Stu cried.

'Yes, you can. Help me pick him up, someone. Come on.'

'I can't fucking move!' Stuart insisted.

He complained of pains in his chest where he'd been assaulted and kept repeating that he didn't know where he was. Then, as Karl pulled him away, Stuart was attacked again and this time everyone heard him being walloped for a second time. It was a definite hit fully on his chest. He even lost a shoe in all the violent confusion.

Stuart was screaming and curled in a foetal position, protecting his head. Karl somehow managed to pull him back from the scene of the attack, but Stu was utterly broken by what had happened to him and he apologised for crying as he tried to make sense of it all.

'What the hell was that in there?' he kept asking.

\* \* \*

That physical assault on Stuart was the most relentless we'd ever witnessed on *Most Haunted* up until then, and he had been left severely traumatised by it. But the very first time that I discovered ghosts can harm you physically, and I mean really injure you severely, was in the Edinburgh Vaults. What happened there affected me so badly that I resigned on air.

We went to Edinburgh for a three-night *Most Haunted Live* investigation for Halloween 2006. This was a big show: we were broadcasting live across the USA on the Discovery Channel as well as the UK. It was also our twenty-first *Most Haunted Live*, but far from being a coming-of-age celebration, it turned out to be three nights of unmitigated hell, which eclipsed even the horror we'd endured at Pendle Hill two years earlier.

Scotland's capital is a beautiful city and we went into that live event upbeat and full of anticipation. Often called the 'Athens of the North', Edinburgh is an exciting mix of ancient and modern buildings, with the magnificent castle looming high above it. It was also a very apt place for us to visit because Britain's first chair in parapsychology was established at Edinburgh University.

Edinburgh has a darker side, however, something that its other nickname – 'Auld Reekie' – hints at. Although the name ostensibly dates from when open coal and peat fires caused thick smoke to hang over the city like a dense fog, it also sums up the old town, which was a labyrinth packed with murky close-quarter dwellings. Life was brutal and short for the masses crammed within its walls. They were regularly ravaged by plague and preyed upon by body snatchers like Burke and Hare, who sold a continuous supply of fresh corpses to medical schools for dissection.

Small wonder, then, that notorious literary characters like Jekyll and Hyde and even Frankenstein and his monster were inspired by Edinburgh's dark history. And under the cobbled streets, deep below the city, lies one of the most terrifying and active locations we've ever visited: the Edinburgh Vaults.

The vaults are a series of tunnels and chambers beneath the 19 arches of Edinburgh's South Bridge. Built in the late eighteenth century originally as storage space and workshops, they eventually fell into disuse and were abandoned. The dark, dank and decidedly sinister vaults became home to the poor underclass who crowded into the old town and became associated with squalor, crime and brutal murder. Those people lived in conditions of decay we can't imagine today. They existed in almost perpetual darkness because there was no light down there. There was no sanitation so they only breathed in the stench of sewage. All the diseases of poverty were rife, as was prostitution, with boys as well as girls selling their filthy, emaciated bodies for a few pennies to survive.

The squalor and despair of those poor souls had seeped into the fabric of the Edinburgh Vaults, and it's no wonder to me that the location is full of paranormal activity. Previous investigators had reported highly unusual temperature drops, violent physical contact, an overpowering smell of alcohol and, on occasions, an aggressive male voice with one simple, threatening message:

'Get out.'

From the moment we went down into the vaults, there was an overwhelming sense of oppression and they all felt so claustrophobic, even the larger ones, because of the darkness. It's all dark stone down there; in some places the tunnels are very low before opening into a small room. Then you go from that room down some more tunnels into what looks like a cave. It's so very easy to feel lost and claustrophobic down there. I also felt so far away from Edinburgh's streets, even though I was only a few metres underground.

Almost immediately the violent activity kicked off when one of the team was smacked in the face with a massive stone. A webcam clearly showed that the stone was thrown and hadn't dropped, and that there was no one near where the stone came from. At the same time, we heard a rumble or a growling and tapping. This was just the prelude.

I was touched, as were other members of the team. We heard running footsteps. The temperature dropped dramatically. At one point, we were surrounded by banging. And glass bottles we'd set up as trigger objects smashed when no one was nearby.

Deep inside the Edinburgh Vaults there is a cavernous stone room, which features an ancient stone circle where legend has it that a coven of witches would meet regularly to participate in the dark arts. One of the curators told us that many visitors to the vaults had complained of being scratched on their arms when they came out of that room.

Noting that this obviously piqued our interest, the curator had a warning:

'Whatever you do, don't stand in the centre of the stone circle. And please, please don't be disrespectful because many people have reported strange phenomena happening here.'

I took the warning seriously and stayed outside the stone circle. However, Karl, Stuart and our soundman Jon Gilbert decided they would stand and walk around inside the circle, goading the spirits to do their worst and being very disrespectful.

'Come on, you fuckers,' Karl shouted out. 'Do something. Do your worst.'

Stuart and Jon joined in and their language was just as colourful as Karl's. Mind you, by that point of the night, we were all swearing a lot, more than was usual even for us on *Most Haunted*, because we were so scared deep in those vaults.

'Why are you doing that?' I asked. 'Please don't do it. Don't be stupid.'

They soon wished they'd listened to me.

We had cameras positioned all over the circle; Stuart had been in shot for around 20 minutes and I was standing next to him as I called out to ask if anyone was there.

Stuart suddenly screamed out.

'God, help me out of here!'

'What is it, Stuart?' I asked, alarmed. 'What's the hell's wrong?'

'My back is burning! Get my jacket off! Get my jacket off!'

He was wearing a black leather jacket over a white T-shirt. When I pulled his jacket off –and this is all on camera, remember – you could see blood starting to come through his T-shirt. He ripped his T-shirt off and there were three very deep scratches from the top of his right shoulder blade down to the top of his left buttock. He looked like he'd been attacked by Freddy Krueger.

I was stunned. In fact, I went into physical shock because I couldn't believe this was happening. I'd never seen anything like it before. Stuart had been in that room and in shot all along. There was absolutely no way he could have left the investigation to do that to himself, not that he would. It wasn't physically possible.

Then Karl screamed out in pain.

'What's wrong?' I asked, rushing over to him in a panic.

'It's my neck,' he cried out. 'The back of my neck. Something feels like it's burning.'

I checked and saw that there were three deep scratches on his neck, which had drawn blood. I felt sick. I love Karl more than anything, and to see him attacked and wounded was horrific.

Then Jon Gilbert screamed out in agony. He wasn't standing in the circle at this point but was on the opposite side of it from me. Alerted by his screams, I looked up and saw him crumple to the floor, clutching his leg in agony.

'My leg. My leg!' he kept crying.

I ran over to him and saw that his leg had been cut from below the knee to just above his ankle. That cut was so deep that you could see the bone exposed. He had to be taken to A&E to have it stitched.

That night did it for me. We were still live and I was supposed to carry on. I tried to talk to camera and explain what was happening but I was falling apart and crying. I couldn't compose myself and was struggling to keep it together.

Not even moving to another spot and talking about something else helped; I kept breaking down. By the end of the broadcast, I knew this couldn't continue.

'I'm sorry,' I said, signing off to the audience. 'I can't do this any more. I'm finished. It's over. I can't carry on.'

I had resigned from *Most Haunted*.

# Chapter 11

The team stayed up all night talking about what had happened because we'd never experienced anything like it before. Fans were turning up at our hotel all through the night with flowers, begging me not to leave the show.

The channel tried to talk me out of it as well, of course, but I was resolute.

'I can't continue,' I said. 'This is something we can't comprehend. We're dealing with something completely different from what I expected it to be. I thought ghosts couldn't harm us but this has proved to me that they bloody well can. I don't want to be a part of it any more. And I don't want people I love being a part of it. At the end of the day, it's not worth the risk of getting injured like this.'

I really meant every word. Just the thought of filming another episode left me feeling sick in my stomach. The whole experience affected me very badly for a while.

Karl was understanding and very comforting.

'You need to do what you want to do,' he told me.

However, I could see that he wanted to continue. As one of the men physically injured that night, he found the whole experience fascinating. He really needed to find out even more about the paranormal but he wouldn't do it without me.

As the shock of the Edinburgh Vaults wore off, I wanted to try to make some sense of what happened myself, and I started looking into the history of physical injuries inflicted by spirits.

I discovered that for hundreds of years there have been reports of violent hauntings with scratching, burning and even actual words being gouged into the flesh of possessed victims. It's a very real phenomenon. The more I delved, the more evidence I discovered. I also discovered that a lot of Hollywood movies, like *The Exorcist* and *The Exorcism of Emily Rose*, were based on real-life and well-documented cases.

Reading all this was a wake-up call for me. It was like someone had given me a slap and a shake.

'Come on, Fielding, get a bloody grip,' I told myself. 'You started this so sort yourself out and find out what's going on.'

So I pushed myself into carrying on. It was frightening to resume at first but I'd reached the conclusion that in death, as in life, where there is light, there is dark, and where there is good, there is evil. All the scratching and burning phenomena are simply tangible evidence of negative spirits. I know it sounds awful but I'm almost disappointed now if one of us doesn't get scratched because it really is such compelling visual evidence.

\* \* \*

The first episode we were scheduled to shoot when I went back to *Most Haunted* in 2006 was at Michelham Priory, where we'd made the pilot in 2001. It was somewhere familiar, somewhere I felt very comfortable, and I thought it would be a good way to ease myself back into the world of ghosts and haunting.

However, in addition to capturing a piano playing all by itself we also encountered violent paranormal activity even here for the first time when a crew member was badly scratched. That upset not just me but also the custodians of Michelham Priory. They'd never experienced negative energy like that coming through before and it really troubled them.

*Chapter 11*

The next time we were subjected to really violent scratches was at Newton House in Carmarthenshire, Wales, which we investigated with the rock band Bullet for My Valentine in 2014. That was another incredible investigation and at one point we captured on camera a wheelchair moving by itself. Things took a turn for the nasty, however, when during a Ouija board session Karl was badly scratched again, this time across his stomach, and it was witnessed happening by the lads in the band. Those heavy-metal lads with their piercings and tattoos were really freaked out by that.

'Right, that's it,' I said. 'This investigation is over. I don't think any of us can take any more of this.'

Our gorgeous make-up lady certainly couldn't. She quit *Most Haunted* that day and, unlike me, didn't come back. I was sad about that because she'd been such an asset to the show.

That investigation was a stroll in the park compared with a nondescript dwelling on a housing estate in Pontefract, Leeds. In fact, if I had to name the one location that I believe to be the most evil and demonic we've ever visited, it would be the aforementioned 30 East Drive on Halloween 2015.

This semi-detached house, which looks no different from thousands of others across the UK, is terrifying because it could be your house. It could be my house. It could be anyone's house. Yet what has been witnessed and experienced inside those walls is so frightening and bizarre that it has become renowned as one of the most haunted houses in England.

As soon as you step inside, it feels like going back in time. The decor all dates from the 1970s because no families have been able to live there for long since then. Little wonder, given that we

266

could sense and almost taste a demonic presence the moment we entered. We heard footsteps walking above us immediately after stepping over the threshold. Karl rushed upstairs to see if someone had got in but there was no one there.

From there on in, the activity never ceased. The EVP we caught there was unbelievable. Lots of disgusting swearing and threats which were very bleak.

'Fuck you.'

'Get out.'

'You will die.'

Every type of object you can think of was thrown at us relentlessly. Thrown with force, with an intent to hurt.

Then a bloody big carving knife appeared from nowhere, wedged in between two cushions on the sofa. Footage shot earlier proved that it wasn't there before. Some keyboard sceptics said afterwards that we must have put it there ourselves, so let me put that to bed straightaway. Most of us had been sitting or flopping on to that sofa all through the day. If one of us had tripped or fallen or whatever, they could have been stabbed or even killed. Why on earth would any of us put another member of the crew at risk by planting a potentially lethal carving knife? That wouldn't be fakery, that would be psychotic, and only an idiot would suggest that we'd do it.

The truth was that house was dripping with evil that night and the very worst came later. Some of us were hearing knocking and tapping and horrible guttural voices coming from the EVP when we suddenly heard Karl and Stuart, who'd split away from the rest of the group, screaming in pain.

We raced upstairs to find they had both been burned in lines across their forearms – and both in the same place. They described it as initially feeling like they'd been hit with a whip or riding crop. Those burns were so bad that they became infected and they both had to take antibiotics afterwards.

We'd come across nasty, demonic energies before but never on this scale where the activity was relentless and vicious. After the investigation, I sat in the car on the street outside in tears and reciting the Lord's Prayer repeatedly.

Karl and Stuart were the last ones out of the house. They turned all the lights off and put the key through the next-door letterbox, as arranged. They got into the car and looked back at the house.

All the lights had come back on.

'If they can turn the bloody things on, they can turn them off,' Karl said. 'Because no way am I going back in there.'

Although Karl and Stuart were the main targets at both East Drive and the Edinburgh Vaults – mainly because they'd openly challenged the spirits to harm them – other members of the team and I haven't been spared at other locations either.

At Shrewsbury Prison, I was nearly killed when a crowbar was hurled at me. It skimmed the side of my face and if it had been one inch to the left it *would* have killed me. On another occasion, heavy chairs were thrown from a height and narrowly missed Glen Hunt, who's been our resident sceptic since 2015. Had they landed on him he would have ended up in hospital at the very least.

While we were investigating Codnor Castle, Derbyshire, in 2018, the Ouija board had a simple and direct threat for us:

'Run or die.'

It meant business, too, because later a doll burst into flames spontaneously and Karl's jacket sleeve went up with it. We later asked the Cheshire Fire and Rescue Service to analyse what was left of the doll and Karl's jacket. They found no ignition point or any trace of an accelerant. So we had filmed spontaneous combustion, which to me was incredible.

We've unearthed many violent poltergeists in so many different locations over the years. Each location we investigate has its own story to tell, and the worse the stories, the more violent the activity can be. When you go to somewhere like the Eastern State Penitentiary or a former psychiatric hospital, say, you can feel the echoes of violence and despair the moment you walk in.

That was certainly true of the former hospital in the shadow of Pendle Hill, which we investigated for Halloween 2023. There were just five of us investigating when Karl suddenly crumpled to the floor like a sack of potatoes.

'Jesus! What's the matter? What's happened?' I cried out.

'It felt like something punched me,' he said. 'Right in the fucking back.'

He was completely winded for several minutes, curled on the floor. When we looked, there was a big red mark on his back where he said he'd been punched.

Given the location, horrible memories came back of that terrible Halloween night 19 years earlier when we'd gone in search of the Pendle Witches and the crew had been assaulted and even had red marks round their neck, just as though they'd been hanged.

Not for the first time, I wondered if that whole area was cursed.

\* \* \*

I understand some people struggle to accept that ghosts can be so physical and so they reach for rational explanations when there are none. I have had proper arguments about it with Glen Hunt, even though he's one of my best friends who I love to bits.

I met Glen when I was a guest on his Real Radio show in the northwest in 2014. We clicked immediately and we were laughing throughout the interview. When his co-host went off for a two-week holiday, the station asked if I'd like to be a guest co-presenter. I did two weeks and it was hilarious. The listening figures went up because we were so rude and naughty. I did another two-week stint when she next had a holiday.

Glen kept saying he'd love to come on *Most Haunted* so I suggested he come along on an investigation to see what happens behind the scenes. He came with us to Ye Olde King's Head in Chester and was supposed to be just watching from behind the camera. But he witnessed much of the paranormal activity, such as a TV set turning on and taps running by themselves.

Afterwards, I said to Karl, 'You know, Glen's an experienced journalist and broadcaster, he's just what we need in a sceptic on the show. He's also a lovely man. Why don't we ask him to be part of the team?'

That's how he joined us.

Our arguments are always healthy and we have a laugh afterwards but sometimes when a sceptic like Glen looks for a logical explanation and can't find it, they come up with one that is far more bizarre than just accepting ghosts exist!

We had a classic case of this on one of our recent stage shows. The negativity of a die-hard sceptic can sometimes dull energy

(I call them Muters because they can mute the spirits' energies) so when we invite members of the audience to join us on stage for a little investigation, as we sometimes do, I always ask that they be at least open-minded.

On this occasion, a guy came up onstage and told me and the audience, 'Yes, I'm open-minded and I'm really up for this.'

So he and a couple of other audience members joined us on a little investigation backstage in night vision, which was being shown on the big screen in the auditorium.

We soon started to hear knocking and tapping coming from a thick brick wall. Everyone, this guy included, walked all around the wall and we could see no one was doing it. This is all on camera, of course.

'Where's this coming from?' the guy asked. 'I can't believe it. This is amazing.' He was utterly dumbfounded.

When we got back onstage, I said to him, 'So how was that? Was it fascinating?'

'It was,' he said. 'But I lied to you. I'm not open-minded. I'm a non-believer, a complete sceptic.'

'So how do you explain what you've just heard?' I asked.

'The only thing I can think of is that you placed a device within the wall to make that knocking noise.'

I looked at him and wondered if he really believed we'd gone in there that afternoon, taken the wall down, placed some kind of ridiculous device in there and then cemented it all back up again.

That kind of thing makes me laugh, although I do accept that it's often based on fear. People often debunk what they don't understand. Or mock it. And I've had people mock my beliefs to my face, which I find terribly insulting and disrespectful. I *can* understand the sceptics to some degree, of course. The history of the paranormal is littered with fakery and that's ruined it in many ways for serious investigators. We've all seen those obviously hoax photographs of Victorian spiritualists with cotton wool coming out of their mouths claiming it was ectoplasm. And there's one American paranormal show that I know is faked because the producers admitted as much to me.

That upsets me because it does such an injustice to shows and investigators like ourselves who act with seriousness and integrity. After all, just because there were snake-oil salesmen peddling fake cures in the nineteenth century it doesn't mean there weren't genuine doctors making important medical breakthroughs at the same time, does it?

*       *       *

What our encounters with the more violent spirits have taught me is that evil exists. I've seen it. I've felt it. I've tasted it. And I've smelled it. My God, you never forget that awful pungent smell of sulphur which is always associated with a demonic presence.

I've seen things that defy belief. I've heard things on the EVP recordings that are so disgusting I would never repeat them. And I've witnessed things on a Ouija board that are malevolent and terrifying. I know there are evil spirits out there.

It's the reason I always talk about protection. Whenever I go anywhere that is reported to have an evil presence or has been the site of a murder or suicide, I always imagine myself surrounded in a beautiful white light from head to toe, a bit like a sleeping bag zipped up. I also call out for my dad, my grandmother, my grand-dad and all my other loved ones who've passed over to come and stay really close to me. That way, I feel I'm protected and nothing bad will ever happen to me.

I don't do what Karl, Stuart and some of the other lads on the team do in goading and provoking the spirits into reacting, often by swearing at them and being disrespectful. That said, if a negative spirit harms Karl or Stuart or anyone on the team, I can really lose my temper and confront them. In those moments, I'm not scared at all and it almost feels like I'm standing with an imaginary sword shouting, 'Come on, you bastards, do your worst.'

I also have three things that I always clip round my neck if I'm going to a horrific location. I have the pendant containing some of my dad's ashes; another silver pendant with my grand-dad's fingerprints on it; and my grandmother's crucifix.

One morning when I was filming in Venice with Paul O'Grady, most of the crew had left the hotel and gone on to the location ahead while I was meeting Paul in the lobby to follow on.

As I was coming out of my hotel room and opened the door, I heard a chink on the floor behind me.

'What the hell was that?' I muttered to myself.

I looked down and saw it was the pendant with my dad's ashes that I'd forgotten to put on. It was like he was saying to me:

'Oi, put that on. You're going to need it.'

Investigating the paranormal is one of the most fascinating and rewarding things anyone can do. It can also be very dangerous and it's not to be played around with. There's no rule book when it comes to the paranormal. No A–Z. We all must learn and feel our own way as we go along, and I'm still learning now.

However, I do think that I've become a little bit knowledge-able about the paranormal and can offer a little advice to anyone wanting to study it seriously.

I would urge them to think very carefully before they begin. A Ouija board isn't a parlour game. You can't play with it. If you're going to do it, do some research but make sure it's the right research.

And always, always protect yourself, because evil exists.

It will be waiting for you. Especially if you find yourself at the Gateway to Hell.

*Chapter 12*

# FAITH, HOPE
# AND DOUBT

*T*HEY CALL IT 'THE GATEWAY TO HELL'.

And by the time our night was over, I knew why.

It was March 2010 and we were in Prague for *Most Haunted Live*, which was to be broadcast over consecutive nights from four very different neighbourhoods. That was a first for us but we were always striving to push the boundaries and ourselves to make the best possible shows we could.

Known as the Golden City of a Hundred Spires, Prague is not only beautiful but is also one of the most perfectly preserved ancient cities in the world. You arrive on a twenty-first-century aircraft but when darkness falls you're enveloped in a gothic world of ancient folklore and mystery. Prague's cobbled streets have been home to some of the most colourful and, at times, terrifying characters history has ever recorded, from corrupt, self-proclaimed alchemists and medieval executioners to those most hideous of more recent murderers, the Nazis.

Perhaps most unnerving of all is that Prague is said to once have been home to the Devil himself.

By then, we were into our tenth year of making *Most Haunted* and we'd already amassed some incredible activity. Just two months earlier, we'd had a remarkable five-night *Most Haunted Live* run at the former RAF West Raynham base, which remains one of my personal favourite live events. At one point, I felt something hit the small of my back and then fall to the ground with a tinkle. Then the same thing happened to another member of the team.

When we shone our torches on the ground, we found some bullet shells, which we knew had not been there before. Historians later verified from the serial numbers that they were genuine Second World War shells. That to me was incredible. I still have those shells at home.

We were still all reeling from how active that location had been and had no idea if Prague would live up to that wintery week in Norfolk.

Prague didn't disappoint, although it was the final night when we investigated a church at Houska Castle that really sticks in my mind.

Legend has it that Houska Castle was built over a gateway to hell; a tale that seems to have originated from the thirteenth century when locals reported seeing winged and satanic creatures emerging from a bottomless pit. Keen to deter Satan, the castle was built over the hole to contain him. But that was only the start of the story.

Despite their fears, local people were curious to know what lay in the pit and so during the construction of the castle, condemned prisoners were given a choice: either be executed or agree to be lowered down the hole in a seat. If they did and reported what they saw, they would be freed.

The story goes that when the first volunteer had been lowered quite a way down inside the pit, the onlookers suddenly

FAITH, HOPE AND DOUBT

heard horrific screaming. When he was hauled back up, it was said that his hair had turned white and he looked as though he'd aged 30 years. He died two days later, without uttering a word about what he'd seen.

There were no more volunteers, the other prisoners preferring execution to that fate.

After that, it was decided a chapel would be built inside the castle over this Gateway to Hell. That is where we investigated on our final night in Prague and where I, in my wisdom, decided we should do a Ouija board session.

In the chapel, right over the concealed pit.

The castle itself is an odd and forbidding place. It was built in a forested and mountainous area and its origins remain shrouded in myth and mystery. It stands nowhere near anywhere strategically important or trade routes, had no water supply originally and was built with fake windows and no kitchen. In fact, there seemed little point in anyone building Houska Castle at all, lending credence perhaps to the legend that it wasn't constructed to keep out external threats but to contain the Devil himself.

It was occupied by several noble families but lay abandoned and neglected for much of the eighteenth century before it was renovated in the 1820s. A century later it was bought by Josef Šimonek, the president of Skoda.

The castle was occupied by the Nazis in the Second World War, which only adds to its menacing atmosphere. The Nazis were suspected of conducting experiments into the occult while they were there and may even have been trying to harness the powers of hell to defeat the Allies. If this all sounds a bit Indiana

Jones, it's worth remembering that many in the Nazi hierarchy were obsessed by the occult, including Adolf Hitler himself.

Our Ouija session at Houska was nothing short of terrifying. The temperature plummeted immediately. We heard growling and pounding and thumping from under the floor – the floor right over the supposed Gateway to Hell. And the glass on the board became very active; curiously, it didn't spell out any letters but instead kept going round in a figure eight.

The weirdest and most frightening thing, however, happened after the show was over. One of the riggers – and this was a very tough, matter-of-fact guy – was pulling the cables once we'd finished the live broadcast when he felt someone or something push him very roughly. He fell down a manhole and broke his ankle. We called the paramedics but they had already left.

This was strange because the paramedics are supposed to be the last people to leave the site of any outside broadcast just in case any accidents happen when the crew are de-rigging. When we eventually managed to contact them on the phone, they were already about 20 minutes away and this poor rigger had to wait in agony with his broken ankle until they returned.

'Why did you leave?' Karl asked them.

'That guy in the old-fashioned costume told us we were no longer needed and could go,' one of them explained. 'We thought he was part of your show.'

'We don't have anyone dressed up in costumes on *Most Haunted*,' I said.

They were adamant about what had happened. We were equally certain the man had nothing to do with us.

To this day, we have no idea who that person in costume was.

That was just the start because in the following days almost everyone who'd worked on that night at Houska Castle had something awful happen to them. I heard stories about tragic calamities and personal loss. It was bizarre and inexplicable, and I was terribly shaken, so I called my local vicar.

'Tell me what you've been up to,' he said.

'Well, we've just come back from Prague where we investigated a castle, went looking for the Devil and did a Ouija board session over the Gateway to Hell. As you do.'

'Which castle?' he asked.

'Houska Castle. Near Prague.'

'Oh, I've heard of that place,' he said. 'And I think you need to be blessed.'

So I took myself and Karl to the church. I can't describe the feeling that came over me as soon as the vicar placed the holy water on my brow. I started to sob uncontrollably and he hugged me.

'Everything will be all right now,' he promised.

The vicar did the same for Karl and he, too, felt highly emotional. Then, just as he was leaving, the vicar turned to me and said, 'You must promise me one thing, Yvette. Please don't dabble in any more of this paranormal stuff. Stop doing the Ouija boards. Just stay away from it.'

'I can't promise you that,' I said.

'Well, you know, please try.'

He was being deadly serious but I suspect he knew as well as I did that his plea would have little effect.

\* \* \*

# Chapter 12

We were definitely dealing with something very negative and evil in Prague and the church came through for us by making me and Karl feel better. That hasn't always been the case, though.

Some members of the clergy refuse even to talk to me because they think I'm scaring people by encouraging them to believe in ghosts. Others openly laugh at me.

'Oh, you're that girl who goes around ghost hunting on television,' they say mockingly.

They almost seem to treat the paranormal as some dirty little secret that the church mustn't talk about. I feel like asking clergymen, 'Hang on, what about Jesus who rose from the dead? What do you preach about the Holy Ghost?'

If you dig a bit deeper, though, you start to understand that the church has always had, and still does have, a much more complex relationship with the paranormal than many people realise.

Most dioceses and churches have their own departments that deal with exorcisms, blessings and hauntings. There's even a seventeenth-century cottage, still standing next to a chapel in King's Lynn, Norfolk, called the Exorcist's House because that is where the church's official exorcist lived.

When people believe their house is haunted, the church is usually the first place they ask for help.

We were privileged on one *Most Haunted* investigation to be joined by a priest called Graham Sawyer, who'd been trained as an exorcist at the Vatican.

When Karl approached him to ask if he'd like to appear on *Most Haunted*, Graham said he'd love to but would need permission from the Church to be involved. When permission was granted, that turned out to be one of the most incredible episodes we've ever made.

Graham is a very softly spoken, thoughtful man and he always carries a little silver case in which he has the wafers that are given out at communion as well as a vial of holy water. He was wearing his dog collar for the show and when we walked into the haunted location, we had the whole repertoire of paranormal activity explode around us. There were loud knocks and taps; we were pelted with stones, pennies, bits of lead piping. I've rarely seen poltergeist activity like it and I thought Graham would be shocked by it, but he took it all in his stride.

'Oh, I'm used to all this,' he said, very calmly. 'I get it all the time when I walk into a haunted house.'

We were so excited by what we'd recorded on that investigation but when we showed it to the channel, they said they couldn't broadcast it.

'Why ever not?' I asked.

'We can't have somebody from the Church on *Most Haunted*.'

'Are you being serious?' I asked. 'Just look at the footage.'

'Sorry, but it would be against Ofcom rules,' they said.

It was maddening that the religious element was causing problems. It was precisely *because* Graham was a churchman that we'd got all that activity; just his words, prayers and presence had made the spirits react as violently as they did. I loved all the religious side of that investigation because it brought an entirely different angle to what we were doing.

The channel wouldn't budge, though, and Karl had to painstakingly edit every single frame of Graham from that episode.

ITV seem to have had the same blinkered attitude in the years since ITV2 commissioned *Ghost Hunting with...* Before his untimely death, Paul O'Grady and I pitched to the network several paranormal-themed shows, following on from the ones we had done for Living, that we wanted to make together. We were always rebuffed.

Graham Sawyer was a fine example of a man of God, kind, gentle and wise, and we've met many others. However, not all the *spirits* of religious people we've encountered have been so benign.

Cowled monks and headless nuns are the staple classics of British hauntings and I wonder if the religious turmoil this country has seen over the centuries accounts for that. If you look at the Reformation or the Civil War, you see how so many people were persecuted, tortured and murdered in the name of religion. Catholics, Protestants, Jews – they've all been targeted at one time or another. People burned at the stake or hanged, drawn and quartered just because of what they believed in. Persecution that's always been fuelled by fear and hatred. Our history has often been horrific.

Just because they were priests or nuns did not mean they were nice people and if they were nasty in life, they will likely be so in death and are quite capable of lashing out.

The vile monk we encountered in Oxford in 2008 was a prime example. He told us through a Ouija board that he hadn't followed his orders, had chased women and caught the pox, which affected his face. He was still livid about the way he'd been generally reviled and he was vicious in his hatred of everyone.

Nuns, too, are not always renowned for their kindness. Having been to a convent school as a tiny child myself I know only too well just how nasty and terrifying they can be. I was particularly petrified of one at my school, Sister Ursula. She was such a frightening figure. She would say to all the little kids: 'Who went to church on Sunday? Put up your hand if you didn't.'

We were only infants of about four or five and so, thinking nothing of it, I put my hand up. I was hauled up along with the other culprits who'd done the same. She then produced a ruler and hit each one of us in turn – smack, smack, smack – on the back of our hands.

I thought nothing of this physical abuse at the time. To me, it was just a normal part of school life, but as recently as the 1970s, the nuns were incredibly cruel to young unmarried mothers. Those poor girls were treated appallingly in the Magdalane Laundries. We once visited one of those former homes run by nuns – this one was in England not Ireland – and the negative energy we encountered there was off the scale. The despair of those poor unwed girls had imprinted itself in the stones of that building, just as strongly as emotions that have been sucked into the walls of old theatres, prisons and churches.

Churches are also often incredibly interesting; they have always been the focus of their communities, so all those emotions of joy and despair, all those memories of weddings, funerals and baptisms, have been concentrated within one building. One thing we have discovered over the years is how the spirits of those who were most proud of their churches or had prayed there regularly are resentful or even vengeful if they've been converted into nightclubs or apartment blocks.

One of the most memorable was when we investigated Brannigans nightclub in the city centre of Manchester for the first episode of our second series in 2003. Every week, hundreds of people flocked to the nightclub to eat, drink, dance and generally have a good time. What few of them knew was that the building had once been a religious meeting hall. When it opened in 1910, it was said to have the largest Methodist congregation in the world and they'd listen to the preaching of the Great Hall's founders. Those founders were making it very clear they disapproved of the people getting drunk and girls in revealing skirts who now congregated there in the twenty-first century; the paranormal activity they were generating was as frightening as it was compelling.

Beer glasses had been seen to levitate and wine glasses would fly off the shelves. Sometimes glasses would shatter for no reason. Mysterious lights had been recorded by previous paranormal investigators. People would feel like they'd been pushed by unseen hands or feel something or someone brush past them. Few, if any, staff members would stay for any length of time alone in Brannigans.

It was an unusual location, it looked just like a normal nightclub, but when we ventured upstairs it was still very much a Methodist chapel. It was upstairs where one of the annoyed spirits made it very clear he wanted us out. We were touched and heard footsteps. We even caught on tape the curious sound of a child crying.

That overbearing sense of not being wanted in that space made me call out to the spirit.

'Are you upset by what has happened to your chapel?' I asked.
He indicated he was.

'Does it make you angry?'

Yes, it did. And it was easy to understand why. In fact, I can
see why many people who took such pride in their churches might
be rolling in their graves at what they've become, even if they
aren't haunting them. It must feel like a desecration.

\* \* \*

Every religion and culture has its own version of ghosts or evil
spirits, and each also has its own way of dealing with them.
Perhaps that's why *Most Haunted* has been sold to more than
100 countries around the world. I once remember having a fascinating in-depth conversation with a Muslim taxi-driver. He loved
*Most Haunted* and what we did, and he told me all about the
jinn, the ghosts mentioned many times in Islamic writings.

Of course, what we do in *Most Haunted* in trying to contact
ghosts is the worst possible thing you can do in some cultures, but
it really fascinates me how every religion has this spiritual element.
It really goes to the core of what being a human being is all about.

As for myself, *Most Haunted* has taken me on a very long
spiritual journey that has changed my beliefs totally.

Before we started the show, I was a pretty much an atheist
who lived my life thinking that when you're dead, you're dead.
Sometimes, I'd look out on a beautiful day, at the sky and the
trees, and think that one day I wouldn't see all of that.

Everything would just be black.

That used to really get to me, especially when my grand-mother died. I didn't want to believe that Mary, who'd been such a vibrant lifeforce, was now just surrounded by a black nothingness.

*Most Haunted* has changed all that. I now know 100 per cent that there is life after death, and I'm a much happier person for it.

People often ask me if I believe in hell and they're surprised when I say I don't – even if I was conducting a Ouija board session over what was claimed to be the Gateway to Hell in Prague! Not the conventional idea of hell, anyway.

If I'd had a closed mind, I'm not sure I could have made the journey I've been on and that's what frustrates me most about the scientific world's stubborn refusal to accept the possibility of an afterlife or even to investigate it. I've emailed so many scientists, inviting them to join us on an investigation, and I don't even get the courtesy of a reply. Not even 'You're a madwoman. Go away and leave me alone.' That really annoys me.

We've had a little more success with journalists, even if the angle they take is often, 'Oh, it's just ghosts. That's all a load of rubbish.'

We did manage to get a scientist along for a *Most Haunted Experience* investigation at HMP Shrewsbury, who was immediately engaged when we received solid thumps from under our feet and wanted to find an explanation.

Suddenly, someone who'd previously been sceptical wanted to get to the bottom of what she was experiencing.

We loved that. If science investigated our evidence and concluded that there was a perfectly scientific explanation behind hauntings, that would be wonderful. There is nothing I would have loved more than to sit down with the late Professor Stephen

Hawking, present him with all our evidence and ask him to try to explain where all the knocks and the raps and the voices we keep getting are coming from. I would have given anything for him to experience what we experience because those knocks that we communicate with are coming from somewhere.

But how will we ever know if scientists in general won't engage?

Scientists are the last people who should have closed minds. Surely the question about life after death is the most fundamental one *any* human being wants answered?

However, I do sometimes wonder if there's not something deeper behind science's dismissal of ghosts. I'm not one to air my own political views in public; I think far too many people in the media and entertainment world do. I'm not interested in what any celebrity or sports pundit's politics are and I'm damned sure no one wants to know mine.

On the other hand, when we learned in 2023 that, for decades, the US government has taken UFOs much more seriously than we were led to believe, I did start to wonder if there's been some kind of establishment cover-up about the paranormal.

All governments and religions rule by control and they probably don't want the masses thinking that there might be another plane after this life. If the people start believing in ghosts and UFOs and that God Almighty didn't create the world in six days, where does that leave the Vatican and the Catholic Church? All the commandments and all those teachings would be tossed out of the window. It could throw the whole world into chaos. And our leaders, whoever and wherever they are, wouldn't want that.

I have spoken to politicians off the record who admit they believe in the paranormal but would never feel comfortable saying so in Parliament. So has there been a global cover-up? Are there forces at work that somehow have such an influence that, without them even realising it, people and organisations at a more local level are unwittingly helping the establishment by putting up barriers to research into the paranormal? I really can't answer that. What I do know is that as soon as we were recording convincing and compelling evidence on *Most Haunted*, we started getting pushbacks and being undermined. It started with Ofcom's decree about our investigations, and others, being 'for entertainment purposes only', as a response to suggestions that psychics in the media should be vetted. Then on grounds of religious impartiality, we were ordered by the network to remove Graham Sawyer from an episode that, to my mind, had given us some of the most persuasive evidence thus far.

Finally, just when we were getting some remarkable results from EVP experiments – we were getting actual voices, in fact – the network suddenly told us they didn't want any more episodes.

'Whoa,' I told them. 'You can't be serious. We're getting amazing results. You can't take us off now.'

That was true. We had a lot of our evidence independently verified, but they didn't want to know. Their view was that the audience wasn't interested in research and that they just wanted the drama. We were pulling our hair out with frustration. It was obvious all they wanted now was the tried-and-tested, and admittedly successful, formula of me screaming in the dark every episode. Less serious research and more shrieking had become their mantra. We seemed to be fighting a constant uphill battle with them over the ethos of the show.

Even though we were their highest-rated show that cost them the least to make, Living still pulled the plug in 2010.

Admittedly, our relationship with them was at rock bottom and a number of issues had developed, but I still think commercially that was an unexpected decision from the channel.

It was so disappointing to me and it's one of the reasons I keep banging on publicly that the paranormal is real. It's the reason why Karl and I started the *Most Haunted Experience* events where anyone – believers or sceptics – can come along to an investigation with us to see for themselves that we're not hiding anything and we're not faking it. Tens of thousands of people have already attended the *Experiences* and we've managed to convince many sceptics in the decade they've been running.

Even so, we've pretty much hit a brick wall as far as getting our evidence out there is concerned.

We've got nothing to hide. It does make me wonder if others do.

*Chapter 13*

---

# LIFE AFTER
# DEATH

*I*T'S BEEN ALMOST A QUARTER OF A CENTURY since Karl and I first devised *Most Haunted* and after everything I've seen and heard, after all the knocks, raps, sighs, EVP voices and physical harm suffered by the *Most Haunted* team that I've experienced, I now have no doubt about the existence of ghosts.

I was in my early thirties when we started making the show, and terrified of death. Just thinking about being in a coffin filled me with utter dread; I would really get down about that. I couldn't seek any solace in religion as I didn't believe in it.

But *Most Haunted* changed that entirely for me. I've come to believe in life after death. I think there are several 'planes' that we can exist on. Life is a plane, where we are always learning, and we progress from it to another plane after death. Good people go to a higher plane, which is a much more vibrant and colourful one. Those that have been nasty stay on a plane that is duller and greyer, while the very worst kind of people, the child murderers and serial killers, go to the blackest plane of all.

Very often the spirits we've encountered while making *Most Haunted* haven't moved on for some reason. The most evil are scared to do so, but I always try to help the others to progress, although Karl has never encouraged me.

'They'll be no bloody ghosts left for us to investigate,' he grumbles.

However, I just can't not do it. If they're tortured and need help, then I'll do it. Not all of them do and are quite happy to linger where they once lived. I recall one investigation in particular, which we did with Vic Reeves as our guest at Belgrave Hall in 2003. There, the benign spirit of a former owner of the hall came through on the Ouija board.

'Was this your house?' I asked.

'Yes.'

'Do you want to move on?'

'No.'

'Why?'

'Family.'

It transpired this Victorian man was perfectly content to linger in the house he had once loved so much in life, just enjoying watching the people living in the house after him. I found the simplicity of that haunting rather touching.

\* \* \*

On the weekend of my fortieth birthday, something powerful and personal happened that convinced me utterly and conclusively about life after death.

Karl made a big fuss; he was determined we were to celebrate it in style. First, he surprised me with the present of a Porsche Speedster, which was amazing, and then he said he was whisking me off to a beautiful castle in the north of England for the weekend. When we got there, he had another big surprise waiting because he hadn't told me all my family and friends would be there as well. It was a huge shock to see them all there, but the best kind of shock.

Karl had arranged for my favourite live band to play after dinner, as well as other entertainments, including a magician. The dinner itself was set out almost like a wedding banquet and although he'd sadly died shortly beforehand, I had a place set out for my dad opposite me.

As the evening started, the table started to vibrate and shake in the precise spot where his place was set out and I called out, 'Is that you, Dad?'

The glasses and the cutlery started to rattle and everyone around was astounded. I found it amazing because I knew my dad was there with us. I felt a whirlwind of happiness enveloping me.

Later, during the after-dinner show, the magician invited me up on to the stage to help with his act. This was in 2008, before iPhones became so widely available, so Karl took a photo of me up on the stage with his old flip phone.

The following day, we were going through all the photographs Karl had taken of the party and he noticed a tiny blue ball of light above my head. Neither of us could work out what it was, so Karl put the photo into the laptop and blew up that ball of light. We were astonished to see that it was my father's face. I can't describe the feeling of seeing him. It was incredible. I couldn't believe what I was seeing.

I always show that photograph at the end of our *Most Haunted* stage shows now and I'm including it in this book because I want to convince as many people as I can that our loved ones really are always around us.

## Chapter 13

I've also contacted other members of my family. My grand-mother Mary has come through in Ouija board sessions; I burst into tears the first time it happened because I loved her so much. Brian Shepherd, the medium and psychic artist we've used many times on *Most Haunted* and one of the very few mediums I *do* believe in 100 per cent, once did a psychic drawing of Grandma. He'd never been to our house or seen a photograph of her, yet it was uncannily accurate.

'She's with you,' he told me. 'She's here and is protecting you all the time.'

My grandfather (Pops) has also come through since he passed, as have other friends. It makes me feel very lucky because I know I have this army or protectors of family and friends whenever I'm really terrified in one of these horrible places we investigate.

It's my dad, however, that I'm in contact with the most. I speak to him regularly and he's always with me wherever I go. Every night before I go and do the stage show, for instance, knocking starts underneath my feet. It's a little code he uses to say that he's there.

'Don't you just want to go and rest?' I ask him sometimes.

'No.'

'Is it because you like being with us?'

'Yes.'

'Can you be in many different places at the same time?'

'Yes.'

I've learned so many things about death and the process of dying by communicating with my father, facts that have simply blown me away.

For instance, he's told me that if people go over very quickly in sudden and unexpected circumstances, like in a car crash or air disaster, the soul leaves the body before the body feels the pain and dies. When it's your time, it's your time and you don't suffer. You're gone. Even if it looks to your relatives that you're still alive and suffering, the soul has gone. I find that very comforting and I'm sure others do as well.

Dad has told me that reincarnation does exist and that you can choose whether you want to come back or not. Most people don't because they're so happy.

I've asked Dad and other spirits to describe what it is like on the next plane. The words that always come through are 'blissful', 'terrific' and 'beautiful'. It's apparently a gorgeous feeling when you leave your body, and unlike here, where it is very linear, time is a much more complex and fluid concept there. When I tell people these things, they find it as reassuring and hopeful as I do.

I also find it interesting that some of our personality traits, and even the things we like, endure after we die. If you're a bit cheeky in life, you will be in death. My dad certainly is. He came through once while I was with my old friend Joyce who is, shall we say, rather well endowed. He was knocking away, as he does, and I called out to him:

'Do you remember my friend Joyce, Dad?'

He tapped out 'Yes.'

'Do you have a message for her?'

He did. And then he spelled it out.

'Nice tits.'

Death hasn't changed his sense of humour at all. He would have done just that in life and then fallen about laughing.

I find that so reassuring.

\* \* \*

Karl and I share our Tudor home in Cheshire today with several active ghosts who seem happy with us being there. The house is very higgledy-piggledy and you've got to bend your head to get under some of the beams. It has so many layers of history, which I love, and although the ghosts have often made their presence known they all seem benign spirits and aren't at all threatening. I often find it comforting to know that I'm not alone there.

Once, when I was at home alone, I found I couldn't get in through the kitchen door. I pushed and pushed and eventually forced it open to find that a chair had been wedged up against it. Then I saw that all the other heavy chairs were in a pyramid, stacked on top of each other. It was so incredible that I took a photograph of it.

We get knocks at the door, but there's no one there when we answer it. The first week we lived in the house, Karl was watching TV when he saw a man in full Cavalier outfit walking past the window.

'Why's there a man in fancy dress walking about outside?' he asked, puzzled.

He went out to see who it was but, of course, there was no one there. We subsequently discovered that the ghost of a Cavalier has often been seen at the house and is allegedly the spirit of Richard Deacon, murdered by the Roundheads who shot him there during the Civil War. That story gained credence when we found some musket balls while renovating part of the house. I'm sure Richard feels relaxed with us living there because I despise Oliver Cromwell as much as he presumably did!

There's also a lady who haunts our stairs. She is always seen in a white dress. I believe it was her house at one point and she's just continued living there. Every so often our paths will cross; she'll see me and I'll see her, although I have only seen her skirt really. Other people have seen her in more detail than I have.

A friend of mine, a stylist, saw her very clearly once. We were sorting through some of my clothes and I had my back to the staircase.

'Oh!' she suddenly cried out.

'What's wrong?' I asked.

She had tears in her eyes as she said, 'I've just seen a lady in full Victorian dress. It was white and she was just walking up the stairs.'

There was no doubt at all in her mind she had seen our ghost and it really affected her emotionally because she'd never seen anything like that before.

Our most active ghosts, though, are our two spirit children, Elizabeth and Benjamin, who lived here in the eighteenth century and who we often hear giggling and laughing. They love to play tricks on us.

We were doing a séance the week before one Christmas and Elizabeth and Benjamin came through. We heard the dogs barking in the kitchen and when we opened the door from the dining room that leads through to the kitchen we found that a chair had been put on top of the countertop.

And those are big, heavy wooden chairs.

'That's incredible,' Karl said.

'Thank you, you're wonderful,' I called out to the two spirit children. Then a thought occurred to me. 'Would you both like a Christmas present?'

The knocking started again. Benjamin tapped out he'd like a ball; Elizabeth wanted a doll.

So we went out and bought a ball and a Barbie doll; the latter was in a box, secured by little plastic ties. We wrapped them up and put them under the tree.

Christmas came and went, and we'd completely forgotten about the presents. It was only when we were taking down the tree that we found the still-wrapped presents, which were right under the base of the tree.

'That's really weird,' I commented to Karl. 'We didn't put them at the back of the tree, did we?'

We were disappointed that Elizabeth and Benjamin hadn't opened their presents but as we continued clearing up, I accidentally put my knee on the ball and it caved; there was no push back at all. We pulled at the wrapping paper and found there was nothing inside. We then unwrapped the doll.

Barbie wasn't in her box and something had undone the plastic ties.

We haven't seen either that ball or doll to this day and it remains a baffling, although delightful, mystery.

\* \* \*

I appreciate that not everyone relishes or even wants to communicate with the dead. That's perfectly understandable. If you do find something strange going on in your house that you don't welcome, the best thing to do is to talk out loud and say, 'No, sorry, whoever you are go away because you're not welcome here. Don't bring any harm and just leave.'

If that doesn't work, then it's time to bring in the Church or consult a professional paranormal group to help.

For anyone who *does* wish to contact their deceased loved ones, however, I always start off by suggesting meditation. I always try to take a little Nana nap in the afternoon and because you don't go into such a heavy sleep as you do at night, I find the spirits seem to find it much easier to come through to you. We all have the capability to contact the other side and our loved ones if we choose to do it.

My dad visited me during one of my little naps and it was the most amazing and vivid experience I've ever had in my life. It was the first time I'd seen him since his death and as I walked into a beautiful white room he came towards me. He was wearing a blue linen shirt, which is what he would have worn in life, and a pair of khaki trousers, like chinos. Although he was 72 when he died in the summer of 2008, here he looked in his thirties and in his prime. He had a full head of hair; his skin was amazing and his eyes were an electric blue.

When he hugged me I have no words to describe that clinch. It was bigger than love. I was so moved because this was really happening; my dad was there and was embracing me. The experience was so overwhelming that I was in floods of tears as I woke up. In fact, I didn't want to wake up because I couldn't bear letting go of him. I didn't want him to leave me.

My God, it was intense and incredible.

Afterwards, he confirmed to me through knocking that it had been a real visitation and that he had come to me.

On another occasion, I asked him to show me what death was like. I wanted to feel what it's like at the precise moment of death. I wanted to experience that for myself. The images that he put in my head were so vivid, so clear, so extraordinary. I was in a car. I was flying through the windscreen like I'd been in a crash. The noise was immense. Like jet engines either side of my head, which was the only thing I didn't like. Then I was floating in the air and I was aware of weightlessness and everything happening in slow motion. There was an overwhelming feeling of love and just letting go.

If you do want to contact your loved ones, for me, meditation is the key. If you keep doing it, you're more likely to open yourself up to the spirit world.

From there, think about your loved ones. Talk out loud to them. That's so important. If it's a special day – a birthday, Mother's Day, Father's Day, whatever – get them a card, light a candle for them, bake them a cake or pour a glass of champagne in their memory. They love all that. I do it as much as I can.

I know my dad is always with me so if I see a TV documentary on something he was interested in, a profile of Clint Eastwood, say, I'll watch it because I know he liked Clint Eastwood. It's the same with the movies he enjoyed. He loved *The Magnificent Seven* – the original, of course – *Kelly's Heroes* and the *Dirty Harry* movies so I'll watch those as well.

'Did you enjoy that, Dad?' I call out when one of his favourites has ended, and he'll knock his appreciation.

'What are you like?' Karl says with a laugh.

I don't mind that because I know my dad's been with me watching and enjoying the film.

I know some people might think I'm a bit mad when I talk about things like this but I don't really care because I know it's true. I feel blessed and incredibly lucky to be able to do this wonderful thing.

I also feel so fortunate to be able to share all this with others. Karl and I are very keen to use the techniques we've learned over the past two decades to help as many others as we can. So we invite friends – or anyone who has heard of what we do privately – over to our house. There, we sit quietly and I ask my dad to act almost like a go-between for our guest and whoever they wish to speak to.

When someone comes through, we urge our guest to talk to them and to ask specific questions to get the validation that they really are speaking to their departed loved one. It could be anything, from which song did they used to sing together when they were in the car or what was their favourite food. Anything that will convince them they are speaking to their grandma or whoever.

When Kirsten Jones from the *Daily Mirror* visited us in October 2022, her late mother tapped out the name of their favourite comedian, Victoria Wood. It convinced Kirsten that she was, indeed, talking to her mum. There was no doubt in her mind. Although she was in floods of tears, Kirsten loved it and wrote about it in the paper.

We have done a lot of sessions like that. It's particularly moving for those who have lost a relative through suicide. Those sessions help people with their grief by giving them closure and letting them get on with their lives. Speaking with spirits is a blessing and it's so important to me to give people comfort that their loved ones are at peace. They're not gone; they're in paradise but they're also with you.

I believe that last point is very important. We don't seek people out; they always come to us. Nor do we charge a penny for what we do. We're not into that. We do it for the love of helping other people and bringing them solace.

\* \* \*

I was asked recently what I think my legacy will be. I'm not sure I'll have one as such, although I'd like to think that I've given my kids and the fans of *Most Haunted* the gift of knowing that there is life after death. I'm very proud of that.

*Most Haunted* has taken up a great deal of my adult life. Karl's, too. That fortune teller who predicted I would work constantly with the man I was to marry was spookily accurate.

*Most Haunted* has evolved a lot since Karl and I devised it. From that first series of half-hour episodes, we've had the lives, the American shows, the *Most Haunted Experience*, and a theatre show which sells out at every venue we go to. We've moved from Living TV to Really, and after Really were taken over by the Discovery channel in 2019 and they opted to show their own American-produced paranormal shows, we started to broadcast *Most Haunted* episodes on our official YouTube channel, where we have far greater control. We no longer use mediums and have a much tighter investigation team.

And yet the essential DNA of *Most Haunted* that makes it work was established right with that very first series. The episodes we make now still have their roots in those we made over 20 years ago because the DNA of the show is Karl and me. We are entwined with and embedded in *Most Haunted*. We created it. We're part of it. I don't think we'll ever be parted.

We started filming in 2001 and we're still filming. I'm proud that *Most Haunted* has been sold to over 100 territories, and we've been all over the world with it, everywhere from a normal two-bedroom semi in Leeds to being dropped down a well in Transylvania. It's been the most incredible ride.

You might think that after a quarter of a century the audience interest in the show would be waning but, in fact, it's growing. Karl and I sometimes struggle to get our heads round that. It's very different from how we started, of course. People still love watching the shows, but then to find out they can go and visit that location and investigate it with the team on the *Most Haunted Experience* is fantastic for them. After that, they can come and see us in the stage show which, again, they love. All variants of *Most Haunted* run hand in hand.

However, I believe the fans like watching the TV shows most of all, and Karl and I certainly love filming our investigations. That's the reason why we'll keep making the shows while he can keep editing them. We've been on this incredible journey together and he still never fails to amaze me with his energy.

He'll sit tirelessly in the editing room, making each show as good as it can possibly be. He never gives himself a break because he wants it to be right. Then he'll go off and do a *Most Haunted Experience* and meet all the fans.

Karl's a fantastic human being and I think we make a powerful team when we're together. We've never made *Most Haunted* for the money; we do it because we adore it. Right from the very start it was a passion for both of us.

'You know, Yvette,' Karl said to me recently, 'I think I'm addicted to *Most Haunted*.'

'Yes,' I replied. 'I think we both are.'

Not a week goes by without us wondering where we should investigate next. How cool is that, to keep doing something and keep loving it? But that's the key to success, I believe: to love what you're doing and to be content with the way you're doing it.

I believe our fans are addicted to the show, as well. Many became hooked with our very first episode. Some of those now bring their children to the *Most Haunted Experience* events and we have a new generation of fans.

It's been a privilege to make the show and it continues to be so. So if I leave any legacy at all, perhaps *Most Haunted* will be it.

As for death, I don't fear it at all. My dad has shown me what it's like to die and it's beautiful. If I do ever come back as a ghost, I think I'll be a mischievous one to have a laugh with Mary.

No one should worry about running into old friends who've stabbed them in the back or bitter ex-partners on the next, higher plane because it's a place all about love and peace and happiness. There are no egos there. No negativity whatsoever. You don't cling to those things when you pass over; instead, you become a spiritual creature filled with love.

It's nothing like this plane at all. Here, our souls are supposed to learn lessons before we die.

This is a beautiful planet and when we cross over, we see it differently. The trees are more vibrant, the skies more colourful. Everything is just richer and more peaceful. That's my belief and I see nothing to fear about that. I'm a much happier person knowing for certain that there is life after death, that I'll be with my dad and my grandmother Mary and all my other relatives, and that I'll be joined by Karl and my children and all my other loved ones.

To be certain of the knowledge that you will go on somewhere else after death is the greatest comfort in life.

*Most Haunted* has given me that.

My journey has taken me from a teenager walking into the BBC who feared everyone to the strong, content and happy woman I am today. I don't look back in anger, nor do I bear any grudges to anyone. Not even to those who have bullied me or let me down. They too have been part of my story and helped make me who I am now. I am the sum of all my experiences, good and bad.

As for where this remarkable adventure takes me next, who knows?

I can't wait to find out.

# ACKNOWLEDGEMENTS

Firstly, I'd like to thank my husband, Karl, and daughter Mary for helping me with this book. During the process we shared many memories and lots of laughter. You're everything to me.

Of course, a big thank you to my co-writer Martin Sterling. He had to listen to me drone on and on about my life. Not once did I see him hide a yawn. He was a brave man taking on this project, but what a joy it was to work together. Here's to more my lovely friend!

I have to give a huge thanks to all my beautiful friends who have taken me back down memory lane. It was an absolute joy to sit with them over a bottle of wine and go back in time. But there are two of them in particular that I have badgered about my past and they helped no end.

So, Joyce Maquoid Taylor, thank you for the laughter and joy you have brought into my life. From those early years in college to our trips out today. Every tearoom should be put on alert when they see us coming.

Angela Sidall. My beautiful friend of many years. I thank you for being there always. You're the sister I always wanted. I love you.

To all my friends, thank you for being there. You really are the best. You know who you are.

Thank you to my dear friend Mark Curry who has always been there when I needed him. A truly beautiful soul.

Thank you to my agent Kate Walsh of United Agents. We hit it off from the start. And, more importantly, you took my ideas and ran with them like a sprinter off the starting blocks. Here's to many years of spooktacular fun.

A massive thank you to Lorna Russell at Ebury Spotlight. I remember our first meeting; you were so excited about the book, I couldn't wait to get started. You were the driving force behind this project. What a joy!

To Abigail Le Marquand-Brown, thank you my love for being the roving eye and having to delve through all my dusty photographs. Your enthusiasm was infectious.

Thank you to Shelise Robertson, Patsy O'Neill and Howard Watson for all your hard work on the book. So much appreciation.

Thanks to all at Ebury. What a calm, wonderful adventure. Much love to you all.

And finally, to my old friend, Ian Thraves. A huge thank you for making me look nice on the front and back of this book.